Populating Heaven

Ron Steele

The ongoing story

of

Reinhard Bonnke's

miracle ministry

Sovereign World

Sovereign World Ltd
P.O. Box 17
Chichester PO20 6RY
England

ISBN 1 85240 005 6

Typesetting by M. R. Reprographics
Chard, Somerset.

"In the last days, God says, I will pour out My Spirit on all people ... I will show wonders in heaven above and signs on the earth below ... and everyone who calls upon the Name of the Lord will be saved." (Acts 2:17, 19, 21 NIV).

Acknowledgements

My special thanks and appreciation to Reinhard Bonnke, Peter Vandenberg and all those beloved members of Christ for all Nations. You've all contributed to this book.

Contents

Dedication

To my Heavenly Father for giving me Maureen, my most precious wife, and daughters Tammy and Kerrie-Lee.

Chapter 1

The World's Biggest Tent

AFRICA has for years been known as the Dark Continent. Today it is also being called the Dying Continent.

Famine and disease, including the modern-day plague of AIDS, are torturing countless numbers of the 500 million people who live on the continent.

Several of the 53 independent nations of the continent are in a state of civil war or some internal political unheaval.

In the past Africa has experienced the imperial might of Portugal, France and Britain. Today it is a continent free of those old empires. These have been replaced by bloody dictatorships, one-party political systems and other variations on democracy and, of course, a sinister mixture of socialism and godless Marxism.

Despite its savage beauty of thundering waterfalls, surging rivers, tropical jungles and savanna grasslands, Africa's future is bleak, if not desperate.

Poverty and death haunt the continent, but against this gaunt background comes a cry: "Africa shall be saved!" Not by big business. Not by grandiose food aid plans. Not by some political genius. No, not by might nor power, but by *My Spirit, saith the Lord* (Zec 4:6).

And the man proclaiming this message of hope is

West German evangelist Reinhard Bonnke, who believes he has been given a divine challenge to preach the gospel from Cape Town to Cairo. From south to north, from east to west, across the mighty African continent.

In 1979 Reinhard had a vision to build a tent that would seat 30,000 people and which would travel across Africa as he preached the Good News of hope, peace and deliverance.

Ever since he first set foot on the Dark Continent in 1967, Reinhard became consumed by a holy flame that caused him to make the bold declaration: "Africa shall be saved". At first it sounded like a slogan, but over the years it has become clear that this is the challenge branded upon his soul.

And so his ministry, in the form of an organisation called Christ For All Nations, or CFAN, burgeoned in the heat of Africa's dazzling sunlight.

His boldness to "plunder hell and populate heaven", captured and fired the imagination of Christians who followed the Big Tent project with excitement, tempered with trepidation.

The vision, though, for the world's biggest gospel tent became a reality in 1984 when this gigantic mobile structure was dedicated to the Lord.

The date for the great day was February 14 and the venue chosen was Soweto, on the outskirts of Johannesburg. Soweto, a sprawling suburb of over one million inhabitants has, over the years, made the international headlines because of riots and sometimes brutal clashes between political groups and the South African police.

For Reinhard, of course, Soweto was the scene of some great exploits of the past. In 1975 he launched a remarkable bicycle crusade which saw 100 personal evangelists pedal through the township witnessing and giving out gospel literature. He had returned again in 1981 for a series of huge outdoor crusades which had seen thousands accept Christ as Lord and Saviour. So the choice of Soweto for the Dedication of the Big Tent seemed quite appropriate.

Once the date was set enquiries began to flow in from around the world. Christians who had followed the saga of the tent construction over the years and who had prayed and contributed financially toward it, were keen to attend the great event.

The exact site chosen was situated on the edge of Soweto, with good access by road for those living there and for people staying in Johannesburg and the surrounding suburbs.

The municipal authorities set stringent standards for the tent erection and seating layout, but the CFAN technicians were able to oblige them.

A bigger hurdle though, was raised by certain church leaders in Soweto who decided not to join in, or co-operate with, the planned crusade. Reinhard's crusade organisers spent many days and hours attempting to unwrangle the problems as diplomatically as they could. It did reach a stage though, when Reinhard almost abandoned Soweto as the venue, but a change of attitude and heart came about and a spirit of unity was forged for the two-week crusade which followed the Dedication Day.

The reality of the Big Tent brought with it a need for some long-range planning and professional advertising and for this purpose an outside agency was engaged to design new logos and advise on nationwide billboard advertising.

The Big Tent and its impressive dimensions (its area was larger than a football field and the masts were the equivalent height of a seven-storey building) attracted considerable publicity in the media, both locally and overseas. In fact, a *New York Times* correspondent, based in Johannesburg, found the Big Tent so fascinating that he called the CFAN offices to interview Reinhard.

Although the Dedication Day was February 18, the preparation of the site started before Christmas 1983. The soil had to be tested and then the pile-driving was done for the elaborate anchor system, before the 20 tons of fabric could eventually be lifted.

There was one scare during the early preparations when a torrential storm, accompanied by huge hail stones, peppered the area. Some of the roof panels had not been tensioned when the storm struck and, because of the complicated lifting procedure, the engineers were not able to lower the panels and watched anxiously as the wind, rain and hail pounded the fabric. No serious damage was suffered and the CFAN crew were satisfied that the giant structure would be able to withstand future bad weather.

On February 14, the Tuesday before the Saturday afternoon dedication, Reinhard called a special prayer meeting to be held in the Big Tent from 8 o'clock until midnight. All the technical, administrative and ministry staff gathered among the sea of wooden benches that were neatly laid out under the vast cathedral dome of the tent.

The CFAN team, of about 90 strong, were joined by several local pastors from Soweto and there was an air of excitement and expectancy as the group walked among the benches or knelt on the sawdust floor to intercede for the Dedication and for the coming crusade.

During the evening a prophecy was given by one of the CFAN team in which the hearers were exhorted to walk in humility and in righteousness. Reinhard, obviously touched by the prophecy, emphasised to all present that the Big Tent was not his and neither was it his idea, but was, he believed, part of the Lord's divine plan and strategy for the salvation of Africa.

Then, during the course of an informal address to the staff, Reinhard underscored the need to recognise each other and added that ministries were going to be born out of CFAN. "Ministries will develop out of this Big Tent," he said.

Maybe not many who were there that night recall Reinhard's words, but they proved to be highly prophetic for many of the men and women who stood huddled in a small circle in the middle of the cavernous tent. I don't believe even Reinhard realised just how true his words would turn out to be because, since then, several men and women have gone out, some to pioneer new churches and ministries for the Lord.

As a grand finale to the evening the team joined together for a "Jericho March" around the outside of the tent, ringing it with prayers for the salvation and deliverance of all who would ever step inside the mighty tent cathedral.

The Dedication Day proved to be a gloriously hot and summery day and from early morning thousands of motor vehicles and hundreds of buses began congregating at the Big Tent. A party of 139 Germans flew to Johannesburg for this special occasion and arrangements were made for a translation booth in the tent. Other Christians flew in from America, Finland, Britain and Australia, with thousands more arriving from every part of southern

Africa. One group travelled the 1,000 miles by bus from Cape Town to be at the service. They arrived after lunch on the Saturday and returned to Cape Town immediately after the service.

Officially, the Big Tent seated 34,000 people, but by lunchtime the tent was full and people were still arriving by the thousands. The day's programme involved a praise festival during the morning, with the official dedication service scheduled for 4 o'clock in the afternoon.

By zero hour the aisles were clogged with people and on one side the flaps of the "canvas" were lifted so that several thousand people outside could watch and hear the service. An estimated 50,000 people attended - one of the biggest gatherings of Pentecostal Christians in the country.

Never a man to relish too much pomp and ceremony, the Dedication service was conducted by two men, the late Rev Nicholas Bhengu, who in his early ministry for the Lord, had been called "Africa's greatest soulwinner", and the Rev Paul Schoch, a Board Member of Reinhard Bonnke Ministries in America.

The main message was delivered by Reinhard, but it was not a flowery homiletical sermonette. No, as usual he was after souls and the altar call saw 5,000 people come forward to accept Jesus Christ as Saviour. It was a moving experience and few who were there will ever forget it. Reinhard told the huge congregation:

"When the Lord first spoke to my heart about this mighty tent the spiritual climate was not right, but we went ahead and started the project. It is always best to obey God. Now, today, the spiritual climate is right. Africa is hungry for the Word of God and this

Big Tent is ready to roll through Africa."

One of several foreign journalists at the dedication was Barry Chant, editor of Australia's *New Day* magazine, who graciously made the trip from Adelaide to witness the great event. Afterwards he wrote in an editorial:

"I'm certainly glad I was there. Over 40,000 people jammed into the tent for the great occasion. I have never experienced anything like it. The sight of 40,000 people, of all races, crowding together in one place in the biggest tent I have ever seen in all my life, was indelibly etched on my mind.

"I looked for policemen that one would expect at such an event in volatile Soweto. I saw none. I wished there had been some Australian secular pressmen there to report it.

"Later I asked a few black people, 'What is it like living in Soweto?'

'It's all right,' they said.

'Could it be better?'

'Yes.'

'How?'

'It would be better if more people loved Jesus!'"

Reporting on the Dedication, Barry Chant made these added, poignant and interesting observations:

"There were a couple of divine coincidences at the dedication. First of all, about an hour before the service, a bird found itself trapped inside and flew round and round about the heads of the people. Many saw it as a harbinger of the hovering presence of the Spirit over the meeting.

"Secondly, Bonnke read from Ezra 6:15 in the Living Bible, 'The temple was finally finished as had been commanded by God ...' the completion date was February 18 ... it was the same date as had been chosen for the Tent Dedication!

"There was an electric atmosphere as the service continued. Dearly-loved and well-known African evangelist Nicholas Bhengu led in a dedicatory prayer. His gracious manner and total sincerity was deeply moving. This was followed by a fervent prophecy from Paul Schoch, of the United States. Then Pastor Ed Roebert, of Pretoria's huge 3,000-member church, led in a prayer for rain. (A week later, such torrential rain fell on the tent during an afternoon meeting that it was almost impossible to hear what was being said.)

"And then Reinhard preached. I have rarely heard a man who is so committed to presenting the simple gospel of Christ. He devotes himself unswervingly to the Great Commission. Where others might wander off into other appealing areas of Biblical teaching, Bonnke does not. Everywhere he goes, he passionately proclaims Christ. In this case, his text was a simple one: *'You are to give Him the name Jesus, because He will save His people from their sins'* (Matthew 1:21).

"For 30 minutes he clearly expounded what it means to be saved. Then, a simple story of an eagle which was raised in a chicken yard - a story acted out delightfully by both Bonnke and his interpreter - with the challenge, 'then the little eagle heard a cry from the sky! He knew he did not belong in the chicken yard. He belonged in the heavens! Neither do you belong among the adulterers, among the drunkards, among sinners - you belong with Jesus! Listen to His call!'

"Thousands of people responded. There was no pressure, no emotionalism - just a strong, uncompromising challenge to follow Jesus. They totally

14

crowded the area before the platform. They thronged the aisles. Bonnke looked at the mass of people jammed against the platform, thought of the small number of counsellors (there were a few hundred) and said: 'I think we have a holy catastrophe!'

"It was after 7 o'clock when the service finally finished. What a day it had been! What a beginning to a campaign. What a beginning to a new era of evangelism for Africa."

The event drew considerable international television coverage. An American TV crew spent several weeks filming and putting together a programme which was seen on several U.S. networks. The news of the Big Tent even caused a visiting British BBC TV news crew to visit the tent one night. They took considerable footage, including some healings which were shown on prime time news casts in Britain, Australia, Zimbabwe and other African countries.

The two-week crusade produced a rich and bountiful harvest for the Lord, with 25,000 decisions registered. Numerous healings took place during the two weeks, although in comparison with other campaigns the numbers who received a definite healing seemed disappointingly small.

However, the quality of the people won to Christ was outstanding. As had happened in previous crusades in Soweto, some witchdoctors were attracted to the meetings. One of them, a practising sangoma, Mrs Margaret Mphaga, came to hear the gospel and was gloriously delivered and set free by the Lord Jesus Christ. *Revival Report*, the official magazine of Christ For All Nations, carried the following, written by reporter Betty Lore, on Mrs Mphaga:

"It is hard to imagine her drinking the warm blood

of a freshly slaughtered goat in the initiation rites of becoming a sangoma. But that is exactly what Mrs Margaret Mphaga, of Soweto, did in her past life.

"The small, bright-eyed, soft-skinned Margaret became an influential sangoma after coming into contact with a witchdoctor, who offered her a cure for her asthma. She took the magic potion offered her and was cured.

"After this she was urged to become a sangoma so as to ensure that no future illness or harm befell her. 'I never liked the idea, but I was too afraid to say no.' So she became a fully-fledged sangoma.

"So how did Margaret get to the tent? Well, the prayers of her son and his gentle persuasion were the key factors. Her son, who has been a Christian for 12 years and is a Bible School graduate, had been praying for the past nine years for his mother to be delivered from the evil influence of Satan.

"When he heard about the CFAN crusade he pressed his mother to come along with him to a meeting. That night God touched her life with His transforming power and love. When she responded to the altar call, Margaret took off her witchcraft bracelets and joyfully exclaimed: 'I am so happy I am released from the chains of Satan. After I was saved on Monday, my elderly mother was saved on Wednesday and on Friday my son bought us each a Bible,' smiled Margaret.

"On the Saturday night Margaret brought a huge pile of witchcraft fetishes and stacked them on the platform, making a public renouncement of her old lifestyle and telling the audience of her new life in Jesus Christ."

It was testimonies like this that hit home in the hearts of many thousands who saw and heard of the wonderful changes that were taking place in the lives of thousands of people. The abundant life of Jesus was in full evidence for all to see and the people of Soweto began to stream nightly to the brightly lit tent to take hold of this new life.

Even after the crusade closed, letters continued to arrive, telling of the joy of God's free salvation. Like this letter from Ivan and Philda Welcome, of Eldorado Park. They wrote:

"My husband and I attended your crusade in Soweto on a Wednesday night and we both left feeling like new people. On Friday night I was touched by the Holy Spirit and now we have started a new life together. You see we were both alcoholics and our marriage was ruined. We kept fighting and quarrelling in front of the children ... our home was going backwards.

"But thanks to the power of God that saved us everything has changed. We have not touched a drop of liquor and we are united again as a family. The devil has departed from our lives. We want you to know that we will always remember you and your team in our prayers as you go from Cape Town to Cairo winning souls for God." Thrilling and heart-warming letters like this abound and it is people like this who often become the most dedicated and devoted prayer partners of the ministry. And the reason is simple: they have personally experienced the power of God to set them free and they know that this selfsame gospel will liberate the continent of Africa!

Chapter 2

Winds of Wrath

ON May 6, 1984, the people of Calcutta were smothering under a blanket of hot humid air. There was not even a whimper of wind to bring some cool relief and the body heat of several thousand people crammed together in the grounds of St Paul's Cathedral made the night oppressively uncomfortable.

On the platform Reinhard challenged Hindus to cast aside their gods and idols and to accept the Living God. His shirt was stained with perspiration and his hair clung to his scalp and forehead, looking as though he had just stepped out of a shower. At the side of the ground loomed the ancient cathedral, its sombre outline adding to a certain foreboding that tugged at Reinhard's heart. But he pushed it aside for the moment. He was not going to be intimidated in the city called the "Goddess of Death". He was here to proclaim LIFE! and nothing would stop him. Heat, humidity, or evil spirits.

On that same day, 10,000 miles away in the city of Cape Town, on the southern tip of Africa, a fierce wind was whipping up giant waves which lashed the shores. Ominous black clouds piled up over the world famous landmark of Table Mountain. The force of the wind battered shipping and roared across the peninsula and the Cape Flats. In its path stood a giant man-made structure. It was the Big Tent.

Vicious storms had been battering the Cape for the past several weeks, seriously hampering erection of the massive tent. Earlier than usual seasonal rains had made the preparation of the tent site and sinking of the giant steel anchors difficult, but the hard-working Christ For All Nations team had stuck doggedly at their task.

The towering steel masts were eventually hoisted, and the huge roof panels raised to form a majestic tent cathedral on a field next to the Cape Town suburb of Valhalla. Although the wet had caused delays, the real concern for everyone was the wind. The Big Tent was situated on an area known as the Cape Flats. And it is exactly that - flat, like a giant-size billiard table, swept, even on calm days, by Atlantic ocean winds. But the technicians were confident. After all, wind tunnel tests had proved that the tent could brave winds of well over 120 kph.

Even so, the Big Tent foreman, Kobus de Lange could not help casting an anxious eye up at the huge roof as the winds buffeted it and tugged at the steel cables.

On May 6 the Christ For All Nations team and thousands of Cape Town Christians descended into a chasm of despair when a wind, seemingly charged with the fury of hell, blasted across the Cape Flats. In a wild frenzy of destruction the once proud Big Tent was ripped and torn into a hundred pieces, as if put through a giant paper shredder. Shockwaves went around the world - the Big Tent, less than six months old, was totally destroyed. A million prayers and a million dollars swept away by a wicked wind.

Meanwhile, in Calcutta, Reinhard was chall-enging the demons of hell. He had arrived in Calcutta from attending a Full Gospel Businessmen's Fellowship International conference in Singapore. He had been reluctant to go to Calcutta, but had been persuaded to visit his sister Felicia, who was married to Dr Ronald Shaw, a leading educationalist in the city.

Reinhard arrived there expecting to spend four days with his sister and brother-in-law on a casual family visit, but found instead that a four-day gospel rally had been arranged. Unable to refuse the opportunity to cast out the gospel net, Reinhard agreed to preach.

It was a furious four days, stirring this city of nine million people to shake off some of its squalid and pitiful character as Jesus came alive to thousands of Hindus. A minister of one of Calcutta's leading churches was moved to comment:

"It is many years since I have seen so many people respond to the call to accept Jesus. This is the first time I have seen any evangelist challenge the people to break away from their superstitious trinkets that our people wear."

Reinhard's brother-in-law Dr Shaw estimated, conservatively, that 4,000 people answered the altar call plea and repeated the sinners' prayer, during the four days of the crusade. At the time Dr Shaw filed this report on the meetings:

"On the second night evangelist Bonnke challenged the people to enjoy the freedom that only Jesus Christ can give. He encouraged them to get rid of their many various charms that adorned their arms, necks and waists.

"In obedience many people cut off these trinkets and fetishes from their bodies and threw them on the stage. Handfuls were collected each night and burned. Virtue, to be virtue, must be voluntary and free. Hundreds received the gift of eternal life that night.

"Some sensational healings were also witnessed. A young blind woman was carried in by her mother and both sat at the foot of the platform. When the young girl was prayed for she stood up and she had strength enough to immediately testify of what Jesus had done for her that night. Her eyesight was restored instantly. Her startled mother, seeing what had happened, embraced evangelist Bonnke.

"Then a middle-aged man, stricken with polio and who had struggled with his disability, came up to the platform to testify to God's power that had restored strength and healing to his legs. Another man, totally blind in both eyes, testified to the return of partial sight to his left eye. These testimonies can be multiplied many times over. Each night crowds of up to 2,000 struggled and jostled in the healing lines."

Another remarkable fact about this mini-crusade was the weather. True it was hot, muggy and humid, like being zipped up and capsuled inside a sauna bath, but the expected rains had held off. It had rained right up to the day before the meetings - and re-started when the final meeting closed. In fact, a deluge caught Reinhard's car on the way to the airport, almost causing him to miss his flight to Johannesburg.

When he boarded the plane, his thoughts were focussed only on Cape Town and the Big Tent for by now he had received the awful news and he had a lot of questions on his mind. How serious was the damage? What would he do about the proposed campaign? What about the vision for the Big Tent?

His battle cry, "From Cape Town to Cairo for Jesus", seemed to have a dull ring about it now, especially with the Big Tent, the flagship of this modern-day gospel crusade, crippled and wrecked on the Cape Flats.

Amazingly, most of these daunting questions were already settled in Reinhard's spirit. When a message reached him in Calcutta that he should urgently telephone his secretary at the office in Witfield, near Johannesburg, his mind immediately flashed to the Big Tent.

"I knew, in a moment, that there was trouble with the Big Tent. But in the same moment I had peace. The Lord assured me that all was well," recalls Reinhard.

When he telephoned his secretary, Suzanne, his first concern was to find out whether there had been any injuries. No one had been hurt, but his secretary tearfully conveyed the dreadful news - the Big Tent was totally destroyed. A complete write-off. When he replaced the telephone receiver on its cradle Reinhard Bonnke turned to his sister Felicia and her husband Ron and simply said: "The tent is destroyed."

There was no anxiety. No anger. No real sadness, recalls his sister. "His attitude amazed us. He seemed to have a calmness and serenity about him. He had instant peace in his spirit and knew God was in control of the whole situation," remembers Felicia.

Thinking back on the occasion Reinhard confesses that the peace that filled his heart and mind was overwhelming.

"When I lay on my bed that night I said, 'Lord, I'm worried ... because I'm not worried!' "

That, of course, is a typical retort from a man

whose boldness and faith grow and grow, and who flatly refuses to drift into a mist of melancholy or self-condemnation.

There was, however, a big finger of criticism pointing at him and his grand plan to take the Big Tent across Africa. For several years, during the construction of the Big Tent, some Christians expressed doubts about his vision. Even when it was finished and in operation these critics continued to hound him. So when the "Big Blow Out" came - they rejoiced! It was the judgement of God, they said. Others declared that there was "sin in the camp." Some even claimed that God had blown down the tent because his wife Anni had recently cut her hair!

None of this gabble ever fazed Reinhard, although it sometimes got to the CFAN team who found themselves doubting the wisdom of the Big Tent and the grand assault on Africa. But Reinhard never doubted the commission given him by God to build the Big Tent. His dedication to that vision has always been unswerving - and unnerving at times, even when the Big Tent and the huge transport fleet ate up money faster than a Las Vegas one-armed bandit!

On May 10th Reinhard jetted into Johannesburg's international Jan Smuts airport. The majority of the CFAN team, of course, were in Cape Town, still dazed and unsure about the future. They desperately needed to meet with Reinhard and to decide what to do, firstly about the crusade and secondly about the future of the Big Tent.

It became clear what his attitude would be and what the answers were going to be when he stepped into the foyer of the Witfield office. About 15 of the staff not directly engaged in the Cape Town crusade burst into song as he stepped into the hallway. To the strains of, "We're together again, just praising the Lord..." Reinhard and the staff linked hands and a tear or two welled in Reinhard's eyes.

But the watery eyes were soon blazing with a holy fire as he shared his heart with the staff. All doubts were swept away immediately. The word tragedy was cast out and an air of triumph took over as he boldly declared:

"This is just the start. The devil has overstepped his mark - again! I know in my heart that something fantastic is coming. This ministry walks on miracles."

It was a short, brief speech that set all hearts aflame again. There was no retreating. The vision was clear and the passion to carry the gospel from Cape Town to Cairo for Jesus was even greater. Reinhard Bonnke wouldn't cower or hang his head in despair with Jesus Christ at his side.

During the course of the next few days details of the tent disaster began to emerge. Although the rain had been a hindrance in preparing the site and erection, it had always been the wind which had caused them the greatest concern.

During the course of Saturday, May 5, a few tears had appeared in the roof fabric, but these had been repaired and by late afternoon the crew were satisfied that nothing serious would develop as a result of these minor rips in the roof.

However, by supper time it was quite obvious that the weather was beginning to deteriorate and as the crew finished dinner and wandered back to their caravans and sleeping quarters, situated on the western side of the Big Tent, some of the technicians decided to make some further checks on the huge cream and red-edged structure, which creaked and swayed as a fresh and strengthening wind buffeted the south-east facing panels.

Gerhard Ganske, a tough, deeply-bronzed West German who was in charge of the anchor system, slowly circled the perimeter of the giant tent, checking the steel railway sleepers which were concreted into the soft, sandy ground of Valhalla Park. These were the main anchors and Gerhard was confident they would withstand any known wind force. The secondary anchor system, consisting of a hundred steel rods drilled and cemented into the ground, were also rock-steady. The steel cables, finely tensioned, pulled taut as stronger gusts of wind blew across the open field.

Milton Kasselman, the chief electrician (who was to die tragically in a motor smash in Zambia 16 months later), walked inside the Big Tent, its cavernous size still breath-taking. Wooden benches, balanced on tubular-frames, and neatly arranged in thousands of rows, gave off a smell that made him think he was walking through a timber yard.

He stared up at the high-vaulted ceiling of fibreglass impregnated material and at the seven-storey high steel masts, which appeared to sway gently in the wind. Milton's concern was for the lighting and sound system, which he had been responsible for mounting and wiring up, using miles of electric cable and installing numerous control panels and switchboxes.

Attached to the seven masts and at strategic points near the platform, were the 95 floodlamps, which lit up the enormous auditorium. Each one of these lamps costs $1,200. They were all securely mounted.

In fact, except for the occasional slap of cables against the material, Milton was hardly conscious of any wind inside the tent. The design of the tent was such that the wind was funnelled upwards and there was no danger of the wind whipping in under the dome and building up pressure and thereby lifting it away like an umbrella.

Tentmaster Kobus de Lange and his West German understudy from Stuttgart, Horst Kossanke (also tragically killed 16 months later with Milton Kasselman), also made an overall inspection of the tent, checking out with Milton and Gerhard. Technically all appeared well. The anchor system, the steel masts and the cables were all one hundred per cent. The only area that the men could not physically check, of course, was the fabric, but experts had assured them it would stand up to gale force wind speeds. They felt sure that the repairs made in the afternoon were more than adequate. As the men made their separate ways to their caravans the wind gusted violently and an unspoken prayer rose in each heart: "Lord, look after this tent."

Sleep came easily to most of the team, despite the bright arc lights which flooded the ground as a security precaution. Valhalla suburb, where the tent was situated, was notorious for its criminal element and few people ventured out after dark - especially on a Saturday night.

CFAN security guards quietly patrolled in and around the tent and the camp site. Midnight came and passed and the guards encountered no intruders, although noise, borne by the increasing wind, told of several raucous, and drunken parties in nearby houses. Temperatures began to drop and masses of black clouds were skudding across the sky. In the distance the darkened outline of Table Mountain disappeared under a mantle of mist and fog.

At about 4.15 am some of the men began to stir in

their beds. Outside the wind had become a constant roar. Caravans rocked to and fro and thoughts flashed to the tent. Electrician Milton Kasselman peeped out of a window. Yes, the tent was still there. In his caravan Kobus de Lange had also been awakened by the intensity of the wind barrage and his thoughts and concern were also for the tent. A quick glance satisfied him that all was still well. Nevertheless, he decided to get up and go outside to make a personal inspection.

Suddenly, above the roar and moaning of the wind came another distinct sound, similar to a whip cracking and an odd slapping ... like material flapping in the wind. The security guards came running and within moments the CFAN camp was alive with activity, men and women dragging on clothes and running out into the cold blast of the early morning. A quick glance at ground level revealed all the anchors were secured, but as the men lifted their eyes the once sharp silhouette of the clean-cut profile of the tent was broken. A panel was beginning to tear and flapped wildly in the wind.

At first Kobus and his men were not too perturbed, thinking that it was merely a repetition of the previous day and that as soon as it was light, repairs could be made. However, inside something gnawed at Kobus' heart and he decided to telephone one of the crusade committee members in Cape Town and ask him to alert some of his committee to pray for the tent.

Kobus also decided to telephone Stan Hughes in Johannesburg, who had been one of the consulting engineers involved with the development of the tent. He wanted more advice on how to patch up the tears and to describe to Stan what was happening.

By 7.30 am the condition of the tent was worsening and the rips were getting bigger and more frequent. Kobus was virtually keeping an open line to Stan Hughes in Johannesburg, giving him a detailed report of what was happening.

Shocked and bewildered Kobus and his crew stared at one another. The unthinkable was happening before their eyes - the material of the tent was being peeled off like a banana skin.

For Kobus and his crew their first thoughts were to try to do something - but what? The wind speed at ground level was moderate to strong, but its velocity at the top of the masts would be far greater and it was impossible for a man to climb the masts. Even then, what could they do? The huge fabric panels were now being shredded into smaller pieces.

The appalling truth began to sink in - there was nothing the men could do, except watch the systematic destruction of the world's biggest gospel tent. Prayers were offered, but as a watery sun probed the swirling clouds at about 9.30 am the devastation was almost complete.

The proud tent was gone. In its place was a bare skeleton of steel masts and cables. Remnants of the roof material clung defiantly to the supports in some places, but most of the 22 tons of roofing were now fluttering through the streets and gardens of the suburb of Valhalla.

CFAN team members wept unashamedly. Nearly five years of work dashed and destroyed in less than five hours. It was unbelievable. Yet the stark truth stared at them.

Smashed floodlights hung drunkenly from the masts. Loudspeakers, amazingly, held fast to the supports and suffered minor damage. Even more surprising was the fact that the two miles of timber seating remained intact. For a few brief moments there had been concern that the wind would begin to lift these and fling them around in the air. Mercifully, this potential danger was somehow blunted. The anger of the winds, so it seemed, had been to deliberately savage the tent roof.

For the CFAN team it was an hour of naked dejection. On almost every one of their lips rose the question: "Why?" Half-hearted attempts were made to try and salvage some of the material, but the hopelessness of the scene almost paralysed the men. What would Bonnke say? What would he do? Would the crusade go on? Was this the end of the vision for the Big Tent to travel through Africa?

While all these thoughts raced through the almost numbed minds of the team another group of men were also reeling under the dramatic reports of the tent destruction. These were members of the crusade executive committee, who were responsible for the detailed organising of the outreach.

For nine, long and gruelling months a dedicated and devoted band of volunteer workers had been praying and preparing for the Great Cape Town Crusade. Three hundred pastors and leaders linked together in an unprecedented bond of unity to work for the success of this crusade.

A total of 5,000 counsellors were trained by CFAN staff and a further 2,000 were trained by local churches, so that up to 2,000 counsellors would be on duty during any one meeting. A total of 1,500 ushers were recruited and drilled and taught how to cope with the big crowds expected to flood the tent. Another 60 volunteer office workers were busy day and night preparing and organising the administrative back-up needed for such a large crusade.

Now, as the news of the disaster filtered through, the Crusade Committee began to ask a similar array of questions as to the future of the whole project and the Big Tent.

Out at Valhalla park the wind began to subside and a cascade of curiosity seekers descended on the sports field around the stripped tent. Some laughed and jested. From early morning people had stood at windows and balconies in high rise buildings and lined a nearby bridge which overlooked the field, fascinated by the wanton destruction of the wind.

Among the people who began to pour into the area were hundreds of Christians and throughout the day believers from all over the Cape peninsula made a pilgrimage to the tent site. Hundreds knelt on the grass and prayed and tears flowed openly on the windswept sportsfield. CFAN organiser Sam Tshabalala, deeply moved by the scene, commented at the time: "It was like a funeral."

Press photographers arrived at the scene and the following morning a full-colour picture of the remnants of the Big Tent was blazoned across the front page of the Cape Town Afrikaans daily *Die Burger*.

But out of the prayers and tears there came a wave of love and comfort which rolled over the hard-pressed CFAN team, who had been trying desperately to make contact with Reinhard in Calcutta and with general manager Peter Vandenberg, who was on a business trip in America.

Unable to make contact with the top management they felt very alone, almost deserted, but in the middle of it all the voice of God was about to be heard. The message was forcibly brought at an emergency meeting of the Crusade Committee in Cape Town on the same Sunday evening.

The man who was at the helm of the Crusade Committee and who would soon join Christ For All Nations in a full-time capacity and become responsible for a major international conference, was Chris Lodewyk.

Chris, an ordained minister, and for some years a champion for coloured people's political rights - until the Lord led him out of that arena - was contacted early in mid-1983 to work with CFAN to co-ordinate the various churches in the Cape for the 1984 crusade. He was a man known for his keen administrative skills and organisational ability, having been on the executive planning committees for the Billy Graham Crusade in South Africa in the Seventies and involved in numerous other major conferences in southern Africa. Chris recalls May 6th 1984 very clearly. He was still in bed when his telephone rang at 5.00 am on that fateful Sunday.

"Kobus was on the line and he told me that some further tears had appeared in the fabric and he asked me to notify some of the other committee to please pray for the situation. However, he didn't sound too anxious and when I checked the weather outside I was comforted by the fact that the wind didn't appear to be so bad.

"Sometime later, between 7.00 am and 8.00 am Kobus telephoned again. This time there was a touch of real concern in his voice when he told me things were deteriorating and they were 'getting bad'. But I still felt no anxiety myself. I believed that the CFAN tech team would have everything under control.

"However, I got another telephone call from Kobus at 9.30 am in which he informed me bluntly that the tent was 'tearing up'. For the first time I realised the seriousness of the situation and got my car out of the garage and drove as fast as I could to Valhalla Park. As I approached the tent site I had to come over a bridge and this gave me my first view of the scene. I was shocked. I couldn't believe it. It looked like big flags waving in tatters from the masts. When I reached the ground I saw the CFAN team members holding their heads and crying and weeping as they wandered around, almost as though they were in a daze.

"The whole scene was depressing, and the noise made by the flapping fabric and the whining of the wind through the steel cables added a hellish dimension to the whole thing. Besides the eerie noise the ground all around the tent was vibrating. It felt like a continuous earth tremor," recalls Chris.

The "earth tremor" was caused by the immense pressure being exerted on the masts and cables by the wild flaying at the fabric and the massive anchors were heaving and pitching, causing earth movements all around the perimeter of the structure.

Once Kobus and his men realised that there was nothing they could do to save the roof they busied themselves with trying to strengthen the steel work and cables and kept the grounds clear in case the masts collapsed. But they stood firm and became the silent testimony to the grace of God in the crusade that was to follow in 13 days time.

Although the wind that struck the tent was ferocious many locals, even today, are still puzzled by the fact that the speed at ground level was nowhere as strong as Capetonians sometimes experience. Says Chris Lodewyk:

"There are times when one has to hang on to lamp

posts to avoid being blown over, but the wind that day was not as violent as that. Yet, when I looked up at the masts I can still remember seeing those sinister black clouds swirling around and you could see that in the air the wind was really strong. Like many others who were there that day, I believe that what we witnessed was undoubtedly devilish in its origin."

As Chris stood, with other members of his committee and CFAN team members, the only thought that blazed in his mind was: "It's all over". But ever the planner and committee man, Chris called an emergency meeting for that night.

As the 20-odd committee members sauntered into the boardroom at the Lighthouse church in Parow it was like being wrapped in a cloak of depression. As Chris took the chair his feelings were down and negative. He could see the same deadpan look in the eyes of his colleagues. It was going to be a dry, dull and sad meeting, he thought. It would be like pronouncing the final rites on the victim. The meeting meandered along for five minutes when suddenly one of the committee men stood up and began to bring a prophecy.

From the moment Pastor Dave Onions stood up the boardroom suddenly became charged with a holy presence. The words uttered galvanised Chris and his fellow committee members. From the depths of their self-pity and despair these men were lifted up and, wonder of wonders, a sparkle came to their eyes and a buoyancy of joy brought a jingle to their spirits. The transformation among the men was amazing. It was almost like an Upper Room experience.

If ever a prophecy was "as the oracles of the living God" these words were: "MY GLORY SHALL BE THE CANOPY THAT COVERS THE PEOPLE,

AND THE PRAISES OF MY PEOPLE SHALL BE THE PILLARS." Not one man in that meeting doubted that this was a command from the very throne of the Father God. To a man they were convinced that God, Himself, had spoken through His servant.

Immediately the committee made two key decisions - the crusade must go on and secondly, it must be at the present site in Valhalla Park. There was some debate about moving the crusade to a sports stadium because of the wet weather which always closes in on the Cape in May, but the men quickly checked themselves, with the words of the prophecy still ringing in their ears.

The meeting broke up at 11.00 pm and the transition in the committee was unbelievable. Only two hours earlier they had trooped in, heads bowed and spirits wounded, and now the room echoed with words of joy and victory. But the battle was not yet won. There was still the matter of the weather. The month of May is notoriously wet and the cold Antarctic winds make outdoor meetings very uncomfortable, even more so at night. So the Crusade Committee gave a very incisive message to the prayer chains that were linked throughout the Cape Peninsula: Pray for dry, warm weather.

It was only the following day the news of the disaster reached Reinhard in Calcutta and when he telephoned Cape Town and was told about the prophecy he concurred with the decision to go ahead with the crusade.

On the Friday of the week Chris Lodewyk drove out to the D. F. Malan airport to fetch Reinhard. The weather was cold and damp as the pair motored to Valhalla Park for Reinhard to inspect the remains of the tent. As they drove, Reinhard turned to Chris and asked him what were the chances of getting a break in the weather?

Chris, beaming from ear to ear, replied: "Don't worry, we've already provided the Weather Bureau with the report for the next two weeks!" Reinhard laughed and the boldness of faith rose in his heart. Yes, it was true - they walked on miracles and the cry of his heart, "From Cape Town to Cairo" was going to be a reality. No hurricane or demonic attack would stop the divine vision to see Africa saved for Jesus.

Arriving at the tent site, Reinhard was brought sharply down to earth as he surveyed the ground, the steel masts, stark and naked, poking up toward the sky; the piles of ripped-up roof fabric rolled up and bundled together. Although inwardly disappointed he hardly showed anything on the outside and his usual buoyancy and determination soon rubbed off on the CFAN team, who were reconciling themselves to the fact of the disaster, and believing that, indeed, victory was still possible.

One of the stalwarts in the midst of the unseen spiritual battle was Suzette Hattingh. This one time nursing sister, who had miraculously returned to full health after almost dying some years earlier, and who had developed a powerful and blessed prayer ministry, was leading daily intercessory groups throughout the Cape Peninsula.

Driving herself to almost total physical exhaustion Suzette, exhorted, and sometimes even bullied, Christians to engage in real spiritual warfare. Her prayer meetings are never dull. No Wednesday night slumber party on your knees and a coffee and cake afterwards! No, Suzette wears out the royal carpet to the Holy of Holies, pleading, interceding and smashing down spiritual strongholds of Satan. She charged up thousands of believers to pray and believe for a miracle in the weather.

And a miracle it had to be. But every Christian involved in the crusade clung to the promise of the prophecy that, "MY GLORY SHALL BE THE CANOPY THAT COVERS THE PEOPLE, AND THE PRAISE OF MY PEOPLE SHALL BE THE PILLARS." Other "words" of encouragement flowed and a genuine spirit of expectancy prevailed in Cape Town. But Cape Town was not the only place where spiritual battles were being waged.

From the Monday following the Sunday disaster, the news had spread countrywide. The telephone exchange in the Witfield office never stopped ringing. Caller after caller telephoned in with a message of comfort and strength. Around the country pastors and ministers began to pray and intercede. Like Pastor Tim Salmons, in Pietermaritzburg. When the news first reached him he broke down in tears, but like most of the saints, he soon rose up and ignited himself and his flock to give every possible support to Reinhard and his team.

A lot of the initial concern, of course, was for the replacement of the tent. Was it insured? Was it possible to replace it - soon? Reinhard assured his thousands of prayer partners that all was well, that the tent was fully insured and that a replacement would be shipped out from America within months.

General manager Peter Vandenberg, in America at the time of the disaster, had preliminary talks with the manufacturers and the insurance brokers also gave a positive indication that the almost $1-million claim would be met. This helped boost morale at the time. Later it was discovered that the insurance claim was far more involved and even at the writing of this book the CFAN claims have not been settled.

Meanwhile, a great concert of prayer was encircling the whole country for the crusade scheduled to start on Saturday afternoon, May 19th. Tens of thousands of handbills and hundreds of posters covered the Cape Peninsula, announcing that the crusade was going ahead - come wind, rain or cold. Many locals scoffed at the folly of this announcement and knowingly predicted failure for the crusade. After all who would sit in soaking rain and wind in temperatures touching zero?

Each morning at 5.00 am Suzette Hattingh and her loyal and devoted team rose to pray, after first taking a peep out of the curtains. Morning after morning the same grey, wet scene met their eyes. The weather, it seemed, got worse. In fact, the storms which battered the Cape of Good Hope during the week before the crusade, were described as "the worst in living memory" and Saturday the 19th loomed closer.

On that Saturday morning the skies still looked like a watery sponge, but by the afternoon a few patches of blue began to streak the grey heavens. By mid-day the rain had ceased around Valhalla Park, although rain was reported only a few miles away! Yet it stayed dry at the crusade site.

In fact, the miracle was re-produced night after night, day after day. Right from the start of the crusade never a day went by that there was not some blue "canopy" over Valhalla Park sports grounds. From May 19th the weather changed abruptly.

Warm air filtered in and for the next three weeks the Cape Peninsula basked in the most glorious sunny and warm weather, a fact that puzzled the weather experts, who described it as an "Indian summer". On only one evening was there a slight drizzle, but by then it was a grateful relief, because the hundreds of thousands of feet and thousands of vehicles had pulverised the ground into a fine, powdery dust which rose in great clouds around the field.

As the sun probed through the grey skies on that first Saturday afternoon, the people began dribbling in. Soon it became a stream and by 3 o'clock it had become a flood. Buses jostled through the congested traffic and by the time Reinhard took the microphone most of the wooden benches were filled with people. First day estimates were put at 25,000 people. A spirit of joy and praise filled the breasts of Reinhard and his hard-working CFAN team. The hundreds of volunteer workers were also jubilant. Indeed, the Lord honoured His Word. This was undoubtedly going to be a great crusade and the glory of the Lord was going to be demonstrated to the people of Cape Town.

On Sunday afternoon the crowd swelled to 30,000 with people in shirt-sleeves and umbrellas to protect them from the sun! Monday night, always regarded as a poor night for attendance, produced a count of 23,000 people. The next three nights saw the crowd touch the 40,000 mark.

Kobus de Lange with his busy ushers and security team were now almost thankful they were not confined by the tent, which could only seat 34,000 people! And so the people flocked to Valhalla Park in their thousands.

The second Sunday produced an attendance of 60,000. All were amazed. Everybody was rejoicing and glorifying Jesus. Yet, God was still going to better that, for on Thursday night, the 31st of May, a crowd estimated at 70,000 jammed into the sports ground and on the third Sunday, which was to have been the final day of the crusade the estimate was 73,000. It seemed impossible to stop the crusade and so Reinhard extended it by three more days and on the last Wednesday night (July 6th) God shoe-horned in a crowd of 75,000!

Responses to altar calls during those 19 days of glory were listed as 29,000, with up to 3,000 decision cards being returned on two separate occasions.

The impact of the crusade was tremendous. Cape Town was gripped by "Jesus Fever" and people who were too terrified to put a foot in the suburb of Valhalla, came to see what was happening.

The suburb had a dreadful record for crime and death and its nickname among the locals was "Kill me Quick". Yet during the duration of the crusade not a single case of violent crime was reported to the police. This was confirmed by Chris Lodewyk, who personally spoke to several senior police officers who, puzzled by the sudden and dramatic drop in the crime rate, visited the crusade to see for themselves what impact the gospel was having on the people.

Everywhere the love of God gripped the hearts of people. Whole rows of houses suddenly became Christian homes as neighbours brought one another to the crusade and nightly saw friends and relatives saved by the power of the gospel. And it was not only the gospel of salvation that was evident in the meetings because night after night mighty waves of healing flowed through the crowd.

On one Sunday afternoon Reinhard began to preach on the subject, "What makes a Miracle." He got only halfway through his message when sudden pandemonium broke out among a group seated at the base of one of the masts. Bursting through the sea of people came a man, wearing blue striped pyjamas, a dressing gown and thick rubber boots. He staggered, almost tripped and fell, as he barged forward toward the platform where Reinhard was preaching. Reinhard paused for a fraction, then swung around to face the man and boldy declared: "The cripples are walking". The crowd erupted into a roar - the pillars of praise under a canopy of God's glory!

On one occasion Reinhard was so moved with compassion to pray for a group of gravely sick people who were placed on one side of the platform. These poor people, carried to the meeting on mattresses, were propped up with cushions against the steel storage containers on which the speakers and sound system were mounted. Laying his hands on all of these desperately sick in this area he cried to the Lord to touch their bodies and, within minutes, a man and woman got up and walked and praised God for a miracle in their lives. In fact, the man was so remarkably healed and strengthened that he refused a seat that was offered to him and spent the rest of the service walking up and down lost in wonder, grace and awe.

The platform at times looked like a hospital workshop, cluttered with wheelchairs, crutches and walking sticks decorating the front railings of the platform. Amid this "outpatients" scene the ex-cripples danced for joy. One late evening a young man, dressed in a leather lumberjacket pressed through the crowd and somehow got up onto the platform and asked Reinhard to pray for him.

The young man, with cleancut features and tousled black hair, was in deep anguish and his eyes cried out for help as Reinhard asked him what was the matter. In a whisper the young man confessed: "I'm a rapist ... please pray for me".

Reports, similar to this one, about criminals and gangsters coming to Christ were daily occurrences and knives, revolvers, pangas, blunt instruments and piles of stolen property were turned in by those who found new life in Jesus.

During the last week of the crusade a young Muslim couple were drawn by curiosity to visit a meeting. From when the CFAN team first arrived at Valhalla Park the Muslim community took a keen interest in the crusade, visiting the site and engaging in debates with Christians. When the Big Tent was destroyed some unsubstantiated stories travelled around the world that Muslims had marched around the site and called a curse down upon it. This has never been proved. But what is a fact is that during the crusade many Malay people, who make up a high percentage of those who follow Islam, accepted Christ.

On this particular day this young Muslim couple, obviously impressed by the stories of the healings, came hoping to get Reinhard to give them a blessing as they journeyed on a traditional pilgrimage to Mecca, the holy city of Islam. But the young pair found Jesus in a glorious way as their living Saviour and announced that they were cancelling their flight to Mecca and instead were going to Jerusalem!

An unending string of testimonies flowed from the crusade and churches were bulging as hundreds of new converts were absorbed. Several new churches were pioneered and are still going on with the work of the Lord today. During the crusade, and for weeks afterwards, local pastors spent more time in baptismal fonts than behind the pulpit as new Christians decided to follow through with their commitments to Jesus. One of those baptised on Sunday, June 3rd, was a young woman who told a remarkable story of God's love and mercy.

She lived in a high rise apartment nearby the sports fields. She was married, with one young child, but her marriage was in ruins and felt she could no longer face life. Arriving home one evening she made a decision to kill her child and then throw herself out of the window. Deliberately she prepared herself and her child, selecting a long sharp knive with which to kill her child. Before knifing the child, however, she walked across to the window and flung it open, glancing down at the hard, black shiny street far below.

She stood for a moment at the open window, her attention caught by the sound coming from the crusade, and then clearly she heard Reinhard's voice blare out over the speakers; "Jesus loves you." Something stabbed at her heart.

She turned, dropped the knife and in a flurry grabbed up her child and hurried out of her flat to the lifts. She ran to the crusade, pushing herself in between the press of human flesh, and heard the closing minutes of Reinhard's message. When the altar call was made she was among the first at the front, her young child pressed against her breast. Truly, a life saved from the edge of death.

The loss of the Big Tent, after only one official crusade - the Dedication at Soweto in February - was a great blow to the planning for 1984. (Part of the Big Tent was used in a test crusade in the Black township of KwaThema near Springs on the East Rand in August 1983.)

After the Dedication of the tent it had only been natural for the next venue to be Cape Town, so as to officially launch the Cape to Cairo gospel trek across Africa. From Cape Town the plan was to pitch the Big Tent in the coastal city of Durban in August, and then in November a final crusade in South Africa in the capital city of Pretoria. After that the Big Tent would move across the Limpopo into Zimbabwe, Zambia, Malawi and East Africa.

These plans were dashed by the loss of the tent, although there had been speculation that a new tent roof would be delivered within a few, short months. However, it became apparent that the insurance claim was not going to be settled without a long drawn out series of investigations and possible litigation.

The loss of the Big Tent though, did not seriously hamper the great crusade outreach. In fact, it catapulted Reinhard into a new dimension of evangelism that would reach masses of people that he had hardly believed possible. Although Reinhard has always believed, and still does, that the Big Tent is part of God's strategy for winning Africa, he readily admits that when the roof was lifted off the tent in Cape Town God lifted his vision to a much higher level.

The Big Tent had a seating capacity of 34,000 people, allowing for adequate and wide walkways as specified by fire control authorities. However, in the first crusade in Soweto, the Dedication Day had drawn a crowd of over 50,000 which overflowed onto the grass outside. The crowds, which soared over the 70,000 mark in Cape Town, would never have fitted into the tent. In fact, Reinhard conceded after the Soweto crusade that the tent already seemed too small.

However, by reducing walkways inside the tent it was hoped to put in many more benches and the CFAN team were confident that they would be able to seat 40,000 people when the tent moved northwards into Africa. Extra speakers were planned for outside the tent so that anticipated crowds would be able to hear properly even if they could not get inside. Now all this planning and preparation looked to have been an exercise in futility. But the huge crowds that Reinhard had witnessed in Cape Town struck a cord inside his heart. Mass evangelism was still possible. Indeed, the people of the continent of Africa were hungry for the gospel. They would come in their thousands to outdoor meetings, even if it took a miracle to change the weather!

Of course, there was still the small Yellow Tent, used for years in rural crusades, but this was totally inadequate for the giant city-wide crusades which Reinhard envisaged. The Yellow Tent continued to operate in outlying rural districts during 1984 and for part of the following year. However, its days as a crusade tent were numbered.

Realising that a new tent roof was not going to materialise in 1984, Reinhard decided he had to embark on open air crusades. It was a decision that had the stamp of Heaven's approval because it vaulted the whole ministry into a new and dynamic role that truly would shake the continent.

Significantly Reinhard felt he had to move across the Limpopo. There was some debate as to whether to hold city-wide crusades in stadiums in Durban and Pretoria in 1984, but the pull northwards was getting ever stronger and the target city for October 1984 was to be Harare, with a smaller rally in Zimbabwe's second largest city Bulawayo earlier in the month.

Meanwhile, Reinhard's schedule was still hectic, both in southern Africa and abroad. However, the decision to hold a mass outreach in the capital city of Harare was going to not only shake the Zimbabwean capital, but seed was being sown for CFAN to set up a base there.

In mid-1984 the thought of establishing a permanent base in Zimbabwe was far from the minds of most of the senior staff, although there had been a minor flutter in 1983 to set up an office in Botswana, but this idea had soon fizzled out. The Great Harare Crusade would not only confirm the decision to hold mass outdoor meetings, but it would also dramatically change the whole outlook of CFAN and cause an upheaval in many of the team's lives.

Chapter 3

Harare Breakthrough

ONCE the decision had been made to cancel the Durban crusade it was also decided to postpone the Pretoria crusade from November, 1984 to April 1985. Now it was all systems go for the Great Harare Crusade.

Since early 1984 Reinhard had been champing at the bit to move north. I recall driving out to the Big Tent at Soweto and asking him simply how he felt about the Dedication Day. His reply revealed the deep yearning and longing to evangelise Africa. He turned to me and said:

"You know, I don't care much for all this ceremony. I just want to get on the road and go north. That's what is burning inside of me."

After the Soweto crusade he wrote in a personal message to prayer partners: " ... the voice of the Holy Spirit is calling us across the Limpopo river this year. Yes, we will move into Zimbabwe later this year. Harare is the target city and together with God's people we will throw out the gospel net."

As a warm-up to the Harare crusade a one-week campaign was held in the city of Bulawayo. The results during this brief crusade were outstanding, with the people of the city flooding onto the hired football field and sitting under the blazing African sun. Thousands of umbrellas produced a colourful scene in the middle of the parched, brown grass of the field. During the week an aggregate crowd of 50,000 people attended with 9,845 people registering decisions for the Lord. Again it was a crusade punctuated with some remarkable healings.

A young man brought his blind father to one of the meetings and a miracle took place when Reinhard and co-evangelist Michael Kolisang prayed for the sick. The father and son came onto the platform to testify of an instant restoration of sight and the CFAN video crew captured the ecstasy of the moment as the son, almost overcome with excitement, hugged his formerly blind father and praised the Lord.

The success of the Bulawayo meetings augured well for Harare and Reinhard had a keen sense of anticipation when he flew into the city for the start of the crusade.

Chris Lodewyk, who had more than proved his brilliant organising abilities during the Cape Town crusade, was at the helm for the Harare outreach. His experience and care of detail, brought a much-needed professionalism to CFAN's crusade planning. He set up offices in a converted house in Fife avenue, Harare, which became the hub of the crusade planning. Night and day Chris and a dedicated team of volunteers mounted a city-wide network of counsellors and follow-up workers. Dozens of buses were hired, posters placed and hundreds of thousands of handbills plastered the city. Chris was on a tread-mill of committee meetings, but when the crusade started on October 13th 1984 at the national showgrounds, the backstrain and commitment paid off handsomely.

Also a part of the strategic planning for the Harare Crusade was Suzette Hattingh and her intercessory ministry. The fruits of the unseen spiritual battle waged by intercessory prayer, were obvious in Cape Town. God had heard the cry of His people and had blessed abundantly.

Suzette arrived in Harare early in October to establish a spiritual beach-head. She made this immediate observation: "I found the Christians needed to be re-awakened to intercessory prayer. They had become weary from their much praying during the war days and had lost some of their spark."

So Suzette immediately set herself the task of building up the Christians into a powerful, praying force. She criss-crossed the city in the early hours of each morning to be at specific prayer meetings, teaching extensively on spiritual warfare.

"We eventually built up a chain of over 2,500 prayer warriors. The pre-crusade prayer programme consisted of meetings from 4.00 am to 5.30 am, followed by a second group who prayed from 6.00 am to 7.30 am. Then I would have another session of teaching and praying for women from 10.00 am to 12.30 pm, followed by another session in the evening from 7.00 pm onwards," recalls Suzette.

It was on this sure foundation of prayer that the meetings were built and the praying didn't stop once the crusade started. Not on your life! In fact, the praying became even more incisive and insistent. When the crusade began the intercessors would start arriving at the showgrounds from 5.00 pm onwards and this number averaged between 250 and 300 each night. They prayed for the specific needs of the crusade as it was happening in the showgrounds - the new converts, the sick, Reinhard and his interpreter and any other detail which the Holy Spirit laid on the heart of Suzette as she conducted the meetings.

Unless one is truly involved in intercessory prayer, it is difficult to conceive just what goes on at a meeting and during the Harare crusade I walked into one of them so as to gain first-hand experience. To the casual passerby the noise coming from the prayer hall was like the deafening scream of a jumbo jet. If you dared peep inside you would have witnessed a sight which appeared like pure pandemonium.

There were people spreadeagled on the floor moaning and praying. Some "wailed" against the walls. Others knelt silently while many more milled around shuffling, walking or striding in a huge, circular march. Some clasped their hands in holy posture before their chests, others waved and gesticulated their arms in the air like baseball umpires. To the uninitiated it must have looked like a place of bedlam and chaos. In fact, it was quite the opposite. There was no confusion in the hearts and minds of these hundreds of prayer warriors. They were engaged in the most deadly of all warfares - they were pressing back the Gates of Hell. They were waging war in the supernatural realm.

As I walked quietly through this whirlpool of praying people I was bathed in a warm spirit of love. I was gripped by the dedication of the Zimbabwean people, crying out for the salvation of their people and nation. Tears filled my eyes as I looked into faces of young men caught up with a holy desire to see Jesus made Lord of Zimbabwe.

The people in the hall came from all walks of life. There were women with babies strapped on their backs. A father carried a young child, while his four-year-old son hung onto his jacket as dad paced the floor praying. A prim, grey-haired white woman, handbag clutched in one arm and a Bible in the other, mingled in the crowd. A pair of nuns, certainly far away from the cloistered silence of the convent, gamely indulged themselves in earnest prayer, although I detected some apprehension in their faces at the boisterous of intercession from some of the men, who physically punched at the air.

Many women brought their babies with them, yet amazingly, I never heard a whimper from one of them. They all slept - despite the cacophony of noise which echoed through the hall. Many of these faithful intercessors never even heard the singing or preaching at the crusade as they devoted themselves unselfishly in the "engine room" of the Kingdom of Heaven.

What I have just described was a daily happening in a hall at the back of the main stands overlooking the showgrounds. This pattern of prayer and intercession is now duplicated at all of CFAN's major crusades where Suzette Hattingh and her co-workers, Charlene Harris and Marlene Holtzhauzen are able to travel to and prepare the way. It is a facet of the ministry which goes largely unnoticed, especially when one is confronted with multi-thousand crowds, the drama of the huge altar calls and the wonder of God's healing power. But the victories demonstrated in the stadiums of Africa and other parts of the world are planned and executed in the realm of prayer. It is here, unseen by the masses, that the real battles are fought and won. It is from here that the power of God is being released to make the crusades such a spectacular success - to the glory of God.

If you become a partaker of these intercessory sessions, there is no doubt that one moves into an area of dynamic believing and faith seems to rise within, faith that is bold enough to move mountains - or even attempt to raise the dead.

It was in one such Holy Ghost-charged session that the inexplicable happened. It's one of those incidents not often repeated, but one which had human pathos and, I believe, Divine humour mixed into it. During one early morning session the voices of the saints were splitting the heavens in earnest supplication when suddenly one of the brethren, an elderly man who had been a devoted member of the intercessory group, slumped to the ground - and died! For the dearly beloved brother it must have been like falling through a window and into the very presence of God. For Suzette and the others it was a challenge. How dare the devil come and pluck away one of their dear brothers!

It was a purely human reaction with no-one considering for a moment that maybe the deceased brother had run his course and was more than contented to become a spectator from the portals of glory. The gauntlet had been thrown down and Suzette and the others gathered around the lifeless body and began to raise a storm - in the name of Jesus! It was a great praise meeting. But the corpse remained still and silent. The praise lapsed into tearful pleading. But the body was unmoved - by praise, tears or any other earthly injunction. But Suzette and her band would not let go the opportunity to raise the dead. They remained in absolute earnest that the departed brother should rejoin the prayer meeting. The corpse was also deadly serious - about remaining dead!

For five hours Suzette and a team of intercessors prayed and pleaded, until someone decided it was time to allow him to rest in peace. The police were notified and when they arrived began to ask some awkward questions, especially when they learnt that the deceased had died at 8 o'clock in the morning! It took quite a lot of explaining to pacify the authorities, who were hardly impressed with a simple explanation: "Well, we're Christians and we pray for the dead to return to their bodies." Trying to explain that to an officious policeman is not as easy as it sounds. Afterwards Suzette and her team had to smile at themselves.

Nightly, the Harare showgrounds became the gathering place of thousands of people. Some came to the ground directly from work. Others rushed home to grab a hasty meal and then chased for a bus to get to the showgrounds. By 7 o'clock each night there was a long jam of motor vehicles and people pouring through the wide gates. Reinhard's clear and simple message of salvation touched thousands of hearts. Prayers for the sick resulted in long lines of men, women and children coming up to the platform to give testimonies. The eagerness of the Zimbabwean people to hear the gospel was epitomised on the final Saturday of the two-week crusade when rain threatened to end the meeting.

A drizzle began falling while Tommy Saaiden, CFAN's gospel soloist, was singing and appropriately one of the items was, "It's Beginning to Rain". The drizzle became a sharp downpour, sending several hundred people scurrying for shelter around the edges of the vast showground's arena. However, the majority of the 20,000 people present sat it out in the open, enjoying the much-needed rain. Although it looked at first as though it might be a passing shower, the rain persisted and conditions became quite difficult for the VIPs sitting on the platform.

Reinhard, general manager Peter Vandenberg and some of the crusade committee, huddled under an umbrella for an emergency meeting and it was very much in the minds of the committee to close the meeting and hope for a sunny Sunday afternoon on the following day.

I was jammed in the middle of a pack of people trying to seek shelter, but as the men on the platform debated whether to close the meeting, a few voices around me were uplifted in an urgent plea:

"We want the gospel". Slowly the staccato shouts became a general chant from the 20,000 throats: "We want the gospel ... we want the gospel ... " That was all that Reinhard needed to hear. Prayers were offered to fend off the rain for the service, but to no avail. So Reinhard grabbed the microphone and preached the Good News. The rain pelted down harder, but Reinhard preached harder. His suit was sodden through and his damp hair was clinging to his forehead, but his subject warmed the hearts of the faithful, who sat drenched to the skin on the long lines of wooden benches.

The subject for the afternoon was the Baptism of the Holy Spirit and after the drenching of the rain came the fire of the Holy Spirit when hundreds received the baptism and the showgrounds resounded to the sound of many tongues.

The next day, the closing meeting of the crusade, saw a massive 35,000 crowd fill the arena and spill over on to the tree-lined embankments. In contrast to the previous day's grey cloud and rain the final service was held in brilliant African sunshine, with a rainbow vista of umbrellas shading the colourfully clad crowd.

By the end of the crusade it was estimated that a gross crowd of 300,000 had attended during the 16 days and a total of 31,000 decision cards completed by people coming to accept Jesus Christ as their personal Saviour.

One of the most exciting healings - among many - was that of elderly Mrs Emana Delamani. On the final Wednesday night she arrived at the show grounds on the back of a truck. She was blind and had difficulty in walking. She was shuffled through the crowd and helped to one of the wooden benches near the front. Eagerly she listened to the gospel as it was interpreted for her and when she heard that Jesus could not only save, but heal she struggled up from her seat and made her way forward to be prayed for by Kolisang and American evangelist Dave Newberry, who were assisting Reinhard.

Mrs Delamani remembers standing among many others waiting to be prayed for and when hands were laid on her she felt a sudden warmth and blinked her eyes. At first she saw only what looked like distant stars and then suddenly the harsh glare of the powerful floodlights struck her pupils. She blinked again and then could hardly be restrained as she pressed forward to get to the microphone to tell the crowd what had happened to her. It was a night of great rejoicing, but more was to follow this wonderful healing.

Mrs Delamani returned to her village, 80 kilometres north of Harare, and the next day she told the people what Jesus had done for her. Within hours she was having a revival.

On Sunday morning I travelled with a CFAN video team and photographer to visit the village and see for myself the revival. When we arrived the whole village of about 150 people turned out for a church service. I spoke to the local schoolteacher, Mr Obert Mbaya, who confirmed that Mrs Delamani had been blind for ten years, but "now she can see again". Not only was her sight restored, but on that Sunday morning she danced for joy in the middle of the village, demonstrating that her leg disability had also been cured.

Reinhard was so eager to communicate the excitement of Harare to his thousands of Prayer Partners around the world, that special arrangements were made for a snap newsletter to be printed and mailed after only the first week of the crusade. In the newsletter Reinhard reveals the spirit of the meetings:

"It moved my heart deeply when on Saturday, alone, close to 6,000 people responded to the call to receive Jesus as their Saviour. Of these, 4,398 made a first-time decision. It is, indeed, harvest time. People are queueing at the 'narrow door' to press into the Kingdom of God. Luke 16:66 says it so wonderfully: *'The Kingdom of God is preached and every man presseth into it.'* My team and I are overwhelmed. The mighty vision for Africa to be saved little by little is finding fulfilment. Jesus is alive! He is among us. He is not in competition with other religions or gods - He just brushes them aside and says: *'I am the Way, the Truth and the Life; no man cometh to the Father but by Me'.*

"The Lord has also poured out His Mercy upon the sick and suffering. We have witnessed some heart-stirring miracles. The crowds of sometimes 30,000 were roaring praises to God when the blind saw and on one occasion, so many cripples started to walk that it was impossible to check them all out.

"The news is spreading far and wide. Even the Harare newspaper *The Herald* became a forum for discussion. Some people were fiercely opposed to the CFAN crusade while others responded very favourably. I guess these reactions are Biblical and to be expected anywhere the gospel is preached. The Zimbabweans have received us with much love. There is a lot of prayer and intercession going up. We had our last crusade here in 1980, just after independence, but we all agree that the spiritual climate today is much better than then. The Holy Spirit is moving in and around the local churches very strongly. There are 138 churches, representing 38 denominations, supporting our crusade. The level of unity is high and this is the key to a mighty sweep of the power of God."

One of Zimbabwe's popular monthly magazines *Parade* ran a feature article two months after the crusade under the headline, "WHO ARE THE HOLY CRUSADERS?"

The article was generally positive, although it made mention of the fact that "some major churches were not invited, the Roman Catholics and Methodists among them - and others declined because of the Pentecostal teachings of CFAN". The article then made this interesting observation:

"It was, therefore, surprising to discover that Roman Catholic nuns, as well as members of other faiths attended the CFAN activities. It was even more surprising when some of these people also responded to the altar call."

The magazine writer went on: "When the 'miracle-working' Pastor Bonnke took the pulpit, it marked the beginning of experiences that had to be seen to be believed. The stage was packed with converts accepting Jesus. The new converts were challenged to break away from all superstitions - including ancestral worship - and even a witchdoctor discarded the tools of his trade, which were burnt.

"At one stage the rostrum resembled a 'rubbish dump' as hundreds threw away all sorts of items from packets of cigarettes to lucky charms and bracelets that adorned their arms, necks and waists."

The magazine also spent some time investigating and following up people who testified to being healed during the meetings. Again, it is interesting to read these remarks, made two months afterwards and in a secular-minded publication: "Mr Hudson Chinyemba, a qualified driver with Harare United Omnibus Company, is said to have recovered fully from an injury that troubled him for the past three years. He had been involved in an accident which left him on crutches. The right leg was completely paralysed and he had constant pain in his left leg as well. Mr Chinyemba, describing events which led to his miraculous healing said: 'After prayer at the crusade I felt like I had taken some pain killers and everything began to shape up'. A number of people have confirmed the recovery of Mr Chinyemba, among them Mr Conceloet Kairirie, a superintendent with the Harare United Omnibus Company."

Besides the hustle and bustle of the daily crusades Reinhard and the team were engaged in many, smaller meetings, like the one at a local bank where Reinhard spoke to about 60 members of staff and when an appeal to accept Jesus was made 15 stepped forward. Then there was a visit to the University of Zimbabwe, where Reinhard and colleague, Pastor Kenneth Meshoe, spoke to over 400 students. There was also a few hush-hush meetings with senior government officials and during the course of the crusade several prominent politicians and senior embassy staff from various countries were noticed, unheralded, among the huge crowds attending the meetings.

One diplomat, though, not only came to every meeting, but was personally involved in counselling and leading people to Christ after the nightly altar calls. He was the Chargé d'Affaires of Togo, Mr Koffi Esaw, who found a higher calling in being an ambassador for Christ.

The triumphs during the Harare crusade are best summed up in Reinhard's own words:

"I travelled about 150,000 kilometres in 1983, but I have never seen such a dynamic move of the Spirit of God anywhere like that experienced in Harare. There is no doubt in my heart this is God's day for Africa. We must focus in on God's ripe harvest fields. The key to evangelising Africa is not homiletics, but a massive outpouring of the power of the Holy Ghost. That will break the devil's back in Africa."

Prophetically he added: "In 1985 we will move further into Africa, pressing on until the whole continent echoes to the name of Jesus. May God open our eyes to the things that are imperishable."

Boldness has always been a keynote to Reinhard's decisions and actions and in those few sentences, uttered in October 1984, he stepped a rung further up the ladder of boldness. Indeed, God has opened Reinhard's eyes to the things that are imperishable.

Unfortunately, it is often difficult to keep up with this intrepid spirit of his. Reinhard is a visionary, and although he shares this vision with his colleagues, it is sometimes hard for him to understand why it takes so long to put the nuts and bolts to the vision.

As the Lord has enlarged his capacity to dare bigger and grander things Reinhard has shown a degree of impatience with the mundane, day-to-day functions which are so necessary in an organisation which has grown in size and stature with a minimum of staff, who have been called upon to tackle tasks and projects of great magnitude.

But such is the loyalty of the CFAN team to the cause of Christ, that this, plus the grace of God, have made it possible for them to accept the challenges that confront them in what is a pioneering ministry on a continent beset with innumerable difficulties on the social, political and economic strata.

These difficulties do not go away, but have to be overcome. Reinhard, although aware of these hurdles, is not deterred by them and won't allow his team to shy away from finding ways around any obstacle which arises. CFAN is not a ministry for weak-kneed Christians. It is not a ministry where plaudits or bouquets are handed out often. A nervous young staff member once asked me:

"What does Reinhard think of my work? He hasn't said anything to me." I replied: "Don't worry. Silence is a good indicator. If he didn't like it he would have told you already."

One thing is sure, few staffers got on an ego-trip at CFAN. Outsiders sometimes think it must be a life of glamour, excitement and adventure. True, those elements are present, but larger than life are the blood and guts issues of running an international ministry, which relies solely upon God's people for prayer and financial support. It never gets cosy at CFAN and only the strong survive the rigorous demands of a leader, who is something of a perfectionist, and who simply refuses to ever accept failure or defeat. Reinhard runs hard with the divine vision and those who follow him and the vision often find their shoes wearing out, but the pace never ceases!

Chapter 4

Brush with Death

BESIDES the unfortunate death during the prayer session, another tragedy almost overcame a young British couple, Gordon and Rachel Hickson, who had come to Zimbabwe especially to see and experience a major crusade. Rachel's mother, a well-known British Christian author, Mrs Eileen Vincent, had attended the Cape Town crusade earlier in the year, and her accounts of the event had so inspired her daughter and son-in-law, that the young couple immediately planned to come to Africa to see a crusade for themselves and to help wherever they could.

Late one Saturday evening Gordon and Rachel, who were staying at the Youth With A Mission home of Mike and Roz Oman, heard the sound of a crash and ran out to see what had happened. Two vehicles, one driven by a personal aide of Prime Minister Robert Mugabe, had been involved in a collision at an intersection. Gordon and Rachel, accompanied by the Omans, ran to assist the injured people. Roz returned to the house to telephone for an ambulance and while doing this a second accident occurred. An army truck came trundling down the road and smashed into the wrecked cars in the middle of the road.

When this happened Mike Oman had just

managed to drag out a seriously injured passenger from the back of the government car, while Gordon and Rachel were trying to pry open the door on the driver's side to release the unconscious and bleeding driver. Also at the scene was a young doctor, Ian Inglis, who was driving by, having just come from his own engagement party. He and Gordon got hold of a crowbar and were trying to open the door when the army truck rammed into them. All three were pinned against the car wreck and on the other side Mike Oman managed to scramble away, although for a brief moment his lower leg was trapped under the moving wreck.

The driver of the army truck jumped out and fled the scene, which had now taken on the most horrific proportions. Both of Rachel's legs were smashed. Gordon had a fractured pelvis and the doctor had been grotesquely impaled by the heavy steel crowbar. It was about this time that CFAN photographer Tony Fredriksson and myself arrived on the scene.

Surprisingly, the doctor remained totally conscious and was helped to his car and driven to the nearby Harare hospital. Rachel, in great pain, was also quickly transported to the hospital, but Gordon, in a semi-state of shock, lay on the street next to the wreck for about 15 minutes before an ambulance arrived.

Fortunately another passerby stopped, who was also a medical doctor and he checked out Gordon's injuries and supervised his removal by the unskilled ambulance driver and his assistant.

In the middle of all this pain and carnage, there was still a moment of light relief. I was kneeling at Gordon's side praying for him and assuring him that his wife was going to be all right, when the passing doctor arrived. As he checked for injuries, Gordon began praying in tongues and the doctor looked up at me and asked: "He's a foreigner ... is he your friend ... can you ask him in his language where the pain is? ... I looked into the doctor's eyes and told him that Gordon could understand English and that he was "just speaking in tongues ... you know, Pentecostal people ... " I trailed off. It really didn't seem the appropriate time or place to explain the Baptism of the Holy Spirit!

But whether that doctor or the young Dr Ian Inglis, who was impaled by the crowbar, realise it, the prayers of the saints saved at least two lives. Some young people staying at the YWAM home joined Tony and myself at the hospital where I stayed with Gordon in the resuscitation room. It was here that I saw the extent of the horrible injury suffered by Dr Inglis. An X-ray was pinned on the wall and I stared in amazement at the dark shape of the crowbar which had entered on the side of his chest and exited just above his hip bone. Later on I joined Mike Oman and the other YWAM people in the hospital corridors and we prayed for the doctors who were preparing for the delicate operation to get the crowbar out of Dr Inglis' body. We also comforted his parents and fiancee. Later we learnt that the operation was successful and that the young doctor survived this dreadful experience.

On Sunday Gordon and Rachel, her legs in plaster, were resting comfortably and recovering from their ordeal. Rachel was concerned about her four month old daughter Nicola, who was now in the care of the YWAM "family". Predictions were that her stay in hospital would not be too long. But on Monday morning a grim report came from the hospital: Rachel had slipped into a [CE] coma.

Marrow fat from the broken bones had got into her bloodstream and was beginning to clog up vital arteries. Doctors gave her a five percent chance of living and, even then, she might suffer serious brain damage.

There then began a desperate, supernatural battle with the intercessory prayer groups alerted in Harare and CFAN team members spending hours at Rachel's bedside praying for her. Her parents, Eileen and Alan Vincent, flew out from Britain to be at their daughter's bedside and a chain of prayer was set alight in Britain, when Alan, who is a widely respected church leader, notified the saints.

The power of prayer prevailed and much to the dismay (and delight) of the doctors, Rachel slipped back into the real world and the crisis was over. The news of the accident, and of the young couple's attempts to rescue the Mugabe aide (a senior intelligence officer who tragically died in the double accident), reached the ears of the highest authorities and one of Rachel's bedside visitors was Mrs Sally Mugabe, who spoke quite openly about the Lord. Rachel and Gordon received an entourage of top government visitors, who also assisted in getting the couple speedily flown back to England where a lengthy convalescence followed for Rachel.

Gordon and Rachel, and daughter Nicola, are now back in Africa - as fulltime staffers with CFAN! Despite their grim ordeal they firmly believe that God has called them to work for Him in Africa and Gordon, at the time of writing, is busily engaged as a crusade organiser preparing CFAN's next major outreach, which will be in the beautiful lake country of Malawi.

This accident shook quite a few of the CFAN staff

as Gordon and Rachel had become almost part of the team during the Harare crusade. It was a stern reminder to all that the saints were not immune from the vicious onslaughts of the devil.

In Cape Town the devilish winds had only wrecked property. Here, in Harare, two lives had brushed with death. Sadly, a year later death would visit CFAN.

In the meantime, Reihard's schedule continued. The success in Harare gave him greater confidence to plan further outdoor meetings and he looked forward to 1985 with relish at what the Lord would accomplish. It was now obvious that the Big Tent insurance pay-out was not coming and that its replacement still hazy. But the mass, outdoor crusades would continue.

Another major event that Reinhard looked forward to in 1985 was the FIRE Conference, which had been postponed in 1984 and was now earmarked for October 1985. This ambitious project was, by now, in full swing, with Chris Lodewyk appointed as the Conference Director. He had been given the mountainous job of putting together this international event, which was expected to draw over 4,000 delegates, mostly from Africa. This event is dealt with in a separate chapter.

Chapter 5

Iron Gates of Islam

EARLY in 1985 Reinhard decided it was important to launch deeper into Africa and that a "recce" into West Africa should be planned. Accompanied by general manager Peter Vandenberg, the two men visited several West African nations, including the Ivory Coast, Togo (where they met with the country's president), Ghana and Nigeria.

In Nigeria they travelled to Benin City, where Archbishop Dr Benson Idahosa has his headquarters. Idahosa, a mighty apostle and evangelist in his nation - he has been responsible for the planting of at least 2,000 churches - had met Reinhard many years previously, but this was the first meeting of some significance between the two men.

Both are men of international stature and of very different styles. Reinhard, humble, but not shy, is not a man who indulges in flamboyancy. Idahosa, who studied at the Christ for the Nations Institute in Dallas and who has strong links with Jim Bakker in the USA, is an expressive performer and a man who has a certain presence about him. To the casual onlooker Idahosa appears a little overpowering at times, especially when he wears the traditional, flowing Nigerian robes which make his six foot one inch figure even more dominant. Inside, though, beats a heart that loves God and longs to see the power of Jesus Christ displayed on this earth.

Reinhard's style is to preach the gospel and then to pray for the sick. Idahosa's style is to preach healing first and then the gospel. Both achieve remarkable results to the glory of God.

When the men met in February, it was difficult to predict what the outcome of their meeting would be. Basically, Reinhard was spying out the land. Would there be some caution or resentment? Would these two giants in the Kingdom be able to co-operate? Like two heavyweight boxers the men sized up each other and Reinhard opened up his heart to the ebony-skinned Idahosa.

The vision for Africa's salvation is nothing new to Idahosa, but to hear it again from the lips of this German thrilled his soul. In turn Idahosa opened up his heart to Reinhard. What he shared touched Reinhard deeply. Idahosa was planning a crusade in the Nigerian city of Ibadan, a Muslim stronghold.

Idahosa, usually as brave and courageous as an African buffalo, was approaching the proposed crusade with more than a little trepidation. He'd been to the city before. It was a hard city. A city where Islam was entrenched. He'd never experienced any real spiritual breakthrough in Ibadan. Would Reinhard combine forces with him for a week's crusade in Ibadan?

"That moment the Holy Spirit touched my heart and I responded to my brother's plea. We agreed to share the crusade costs - although I knew that CFAN's kitty was empty. Deep down in my heart I knew that this was the perfect will of God. And so we shared the burden and ministry," remembers Reinhard.

Like little schoolboys the men excitedly looked up

their diaries so as to co-ordinate the meeting. Only one week, in March, was open in both of their diaries and was only four weeks away. Could a crusade be put together in such a short time? It seemed a tall order. But both men felt so convinced that this was God's doing that they agreed on the date and Idahosa immediately rushed his huge organisation into top gear.

On the flight back to their base Reinhard and Peter had time to reflect on the step they had just taken. They had agreed to share the costs of the crusade and it would come to about $100,000 and they both knew the bank balance was nowhere near the six figure mark. In fact, it was going to be a struggle to meet the salary packet for the next month! Still, Reinhard had that unshakeable assurance that he had acted in pure faith, and that there was no possibility of presumption.

Within a few days of arriving home Reinhard received a trans-Atlantic telephone call. It was Barry Hon, a personal friend, who had taken some of CFAN's ministry affairs under his wing in America. Barry, a mild-mannered unassuming businessman with a great love for the Lord's work, doesn't waste words. The Lord had impressed him that there was an urgent financial need and a cheque for $40,000 was on the way! The Ibadan crusade would go ahead.

Nigeria is a nation of 120 million people. In fact, one out of every four persons on the continent of Africa is a Nigerian - truly a nation ready for the harvest. Reinhard, Peter Vandenberg, co-evangelist Michael Kolisang, photographer Tony Fredriksson, crusade organisers Werner Drotleff and Eckkehard Honsburg, as well as Reinhard's 17-year-old son Freddy, made up the CFAN team which spearheaded the crusade to be held at the Olubadan sports stadium in Ibadan.

The visit to Ibadan was a very different experience for many of the team.

Time has stood still in the market place of Ibadan. There are no neon lights or slick supermarkets with steel trolleys for the housewives. Instead the women engage in bartering, haggling over prices, while customers have every opportunity to see the goods at close quarters, whether it be fruit, vegetables or fresh meat.

Ibadan, with a population nearing four million people, is reputed to be the largest city south of the Sahara. It is an old city, consisting of a myriad of small buildings and spreads for many miles. It is older than the capital city of Lagos and in times past was a major trading centre with the Arabs, who travelled down from the north. Early Portuguese traders also paid periodic visits to Ibadan.

The Arabic influence is still felt in Ibadan with 50 per cent of its population followers of the Islamic faith. The other 50 per cent of the population is made up of Christians and pagans.

The lifestyle of these people is simple and there is overcrowding and a lack of basic essentials. A Lagos newspaper report, at the time, gave some startling figures about housing, admitting that only 33.3 per cent of houses in Ibadan have water and only 56 per cent have electricity. But, despite their material lack, the people were open, friendly and wonderfully receptive to the gospel.

Reinhard received a most unusual welcome. Arriving with Idahosa's entourage at the airport, they stepped onto the tarmac to be met by a glittering array of army and police officials. He was then escorted to a shiny Mercedes and found himself the head of a motor cavalcade which snaked through the old and often dingy city. He smiled and waved to the crowd and in the best electioneering style tried to shake a few hands along the way, but it was not Reinhard's style. He felt uncomfortable, especially with the striking contrast of wealth and poverty so obvious.

However, Reinhard was soon gripped by the atmosphere of the city. There was hope and faith in the air. Idahosa and his workers had done a first class job in publicising the meetings and had also bought time on the local television station. The people of Ibadan were well informed about the meeting with two of the world's most exciting and dynamic speakers sharing the platform.

They came in their tens of thousands to the Olubadan stadium. The local newspaper, the *Sketch* estimated one crowd at a half a million people. However, conservative estimates by crusade organisers put the figure at about 250,000. As evangelist Bonnke admitted afterwards, it was the biggest crowd, up to then, that he had ever preached to in his life.

At the first meeting the crowds gave a traditional welcome to the Christ For All Nations team, taking out handkerchiefs and waving them gaily in the air. During the whole of the crusade evangelist Bonnke wore a traditional Nigerian robe (which he dubbed his garment of praise) and endeared himself to the people of Nigeria with his message of love and life.

The crowds, which began filling the stadium in the late afternoon for the evening service, were oblivious to time or the inconvenience of standing in the open field. Only those who came early were able to get a seat in the grandstand. The huge crowds were wonderful, despite the crushing, and stood and sang for hours, praising and worshipping the Lord.

The meetings were truly anointed by the Holy Spirit. Day after day the Word of God stirred the hearts of thousands of people who found the reality of Jesus Christ as their Saviour. Even as the gospel was being preached there were interruptions from the crowd as men and women suddenly exploded with excitement when they realised they had been touched by the power of God.

Because of the massive crowds it was impossible to keep an account of the miracles. Thousands of healings were claimed, cripples threw their crutches away, blind and deaf people were healed. One mother, a Muslim, brought her young deaf daughter to the crusade. The child had been deaf from birth, but Jesus of Nazareth visited her in this vast stadium and she joyfully testified to this miracle. The local newspapers gave extensive coverage to the crusade and reported many of the miracles, including pictures of those who had been healed.

The size of the crowds staggered even the local media and one report in the *Sketch* read:

"As the crusade entered its second outing yesterday, the Olubadan Stadium, venue of the event, was packed full inside and outside. Never in the history of the Nigerian Federation had people gathered in such large numbers for such an occasion. Not even the visit of Queen Elizabeth, of Great Britain, to Nigeria or the historic Independence Day or any political rally has attracted such an indescribable meeting of heads for a single purpose - to be healed and re-created."

On one day the crowd was so large that the traffic

police were left helpless and unable to control the congestion. Two of their officers collapsed from heat exhaustion, as they battled to direct traffic at intersections.

People and vehicles blocked every street for two miles around the stadium. The police told the crusade organisers they turned away up to 30,000 people because of the traffic congestion. Among those trapped was Idahosa, who at one stage leapt out of his vehicle and began to direct the traffic.

That evening, the Holy Spirit swept through the mass of people and miracles began happening everywhere. The *Evening Sketch* reported on some of the healings:

● Adebisi Adeyemi, paralytic, started walking and jumped happily on the rostrom.

● Justina Olu Olaji, of Ile-Ife, had been blind for 25 years, regained his sight.

● For seven years Aminatu Oladele was a deaf mute, but heard and spoke a few words.

● Samuel Esieboh, who had been incapacitated in a car accident, stood erect, walked and jumped.

● Dapo Atanda, a teacher at a secondary school in Ibadan, felled by a stroke, regained his mobility.

The newspaper demonstrated tremendous freedom to report the crusade - unlike much of the secular media in the western world. In fact, the reporter, obviously a Christian himself, boldly commented on evolution theories in the course of his article.

He wrote: "Words of God are hard to believe, for some. There are millions who instead of tracing their roots to God, claim their origin from the ape. I don't belong to that school of thought and neither do Nigerians."

He went on to write: "What is happening in the

state capital of Oyo is the redeeming hand of the Lord - working to remove our poverty, unhappiness and other ills of our way."

Reinhard was featured in a full length, front page photograph, holding a young boy who had been healed of a crippling leg condition. The caption read:

"Reverend Reinhard Bonnke joyfully carrying a young boy who was crippled and brought by his parents to the second day of the crusade at the Olubadan stadium. The boy who walked, ran and jumped was among many disabled who were healed and came to the rostrum to attest to the power of God. The boy's parents who were overjoyous, continued shouting and dancing when we asked for the name of the lad."

Summing up the Ibadan experience Reinhard said: "In all the years of my ministry I have never seen what I experienced in Ibadan. What this crusade has done to my own heart is not difficult to imagine. We at Christ For All Nations are moving out and into the heart of Africa to capture this mighty harvest for the Kingdom of God.

"Hundreds of thousands of people have heard the Word of God. The local newspapers said that never in the history of this city has there been such a gathering of people - not even when British royalty visited Ibadan! To God be the praise and thanks. Yes, Jesus is the King of Kings and He's worthy to be listened to.

"We have proclaimed the Word and the people have been hungry to receive this message of life and hope. The power of God has moved over the people like a wave. Miracles happened while we preached and everywhere the people burst forth with applause when the blind received their sight and the cripples walked, but even more so when people received peace and forgiveness through the Blood of Jesus.

"I have been deeply moved in my heart - God is fulfilling His Word. We will take the continent of Africa for Jesus - from Cape Town to Cairo. There is a wave of faith and power sweeping over Africa as the Holy Spirit does His marvellous work."

Reinhard and his small team were still full of "hype" when they returned to the Witfield base. The size of the crowds and the magnitude of God's power made an everlasting impression on all of them. For Reinhard, of course, it meant that there were still bigger and mightier things to follow!

Although he counted it a great privilege to have been a part of the Ibadan Crusade, Reinhard was not going to sit back and bathe himself in sweet memories. If God could do it once, then He could do it again. And Reinhard was sure that sometime in the not too distant future he would be preaching to a live audience of a million people!

Presumption? Boastfulness? A preoccupation with bigger and greater crowds? An outsider may be excused for raising those questions. But insiders know better. The harvest is ripe. The harvest is very large. Somebody has to reap it. And Reinhard is a man God trusts to net this great catch for the Kingdom of Heaven.

Chapter 6

Racism Challenged

BACK in South Africa Reinhard was to fulfil one last crusade engagement in the country which he was soon to leave. The choice of Pretoria for a farewell crusade - although it was not known then - was apt.

The city has heavy symbolic connotations. Militant international organisations scathingly refer to the "Pretoria racist regime". It is, in a sense, seen as the bastion of Afrikanerdom and the unjust system of apartheid. Just as Johannesburg is the commercial and financial pulse of South Africa so Pretoria throbs out political signals.

Political boffins in recent years have focussed most of their attention on the creeping violence in South Africa, disinvestment, sanctions and the merry-go-round of proposed internal changes and reforms.

Most South Africans, of all races, have a deep desire for peace, harmony and prosperity for the future, words that sound hollow in view of the killings, arson, unemployment and various economic hazards which threaten South Africa. The plea and cry of the nation is for solutions. Politicians, academics, industrialists, and clerics churn out verbiage that is only a desperate echo for help.

Racism is undoubtedly an ugly scar on the heart of South Africa, but when Reinhard preached at the Pilditch sports arena on April 27th to May 5th there was a demonstration of what God's love can do and is doing in this beleaguered nation.

Much of the world's media, ignore the good and concentrate on the bad and ugly. But for nine days the people of Pretoria - mainly Afrikaners - experienced something beautiful. So what relevance does a gathering of saints and sinners have on a national crisis? Everything.

For nine days Blacks, Whites, Coloureds and Indians filed into the Pilditch athletic stadium. They sang together, prayed together, wept together and rejoiced together.

For the thousands of Whites who came to the stadium it was not only a meeting with God, but a social education. Afrikaans-speaking citizens of Pretoria rubbed shoulders, held hands and united in an unprecedented way with their Black and Brown brethren - and found that under the coloured skin was a fellow Christian, who loved and served God just as fervently as he, himself, professed.

During the course of the nine days over 80,000 people attended, with over 16,000 people at the final Sunday afternoon meeting. And church ministers were unanimous about the spirit of unity that prevailed. The ugliness of racism disappeared for nine glorious days.

Why, you may ask? The answer is childishly simple: Jesus. The Man who walked the dusty roads of Palestine nearly two thousand years ago is declared to be the PRINCE OF PEACE. And for nine days this peace was powerfully demonstrated at the JESUS 85 crusade in Pretoria.

There, on the grassy island of the Pilditch sports field, the gospel of reconciliation was practically demonstrated. The masks fell and Christians, Black and White began to see the truth: they were all sinners once, no better, no worse; whether they lived in a slum or a posh suburb. They all needed God's love and salvation.

And they recognised the other truth: they were all born of the same Divine Spirit and forgiven as a result of the same Divine sacrifice. For nine days Christians in Pretoria found they had more to agree about than to disagree about.

Nightly they came to sing, worship and lift up holy hands to the Lord. Nightly, they prayed together for a single purpose: to see the Kingdom of God enlarged. Nightly they rejoiced to see hundreds of sinners turn to the Lord in repentance and find new life, hope and peace in the Lord Jesus Christ.

One night I joined a prayer group. My companions were a Black man, an Afrikaans-speaking White and me, an English-speaking Whitey. I noticed the symbolism of our threesome and thanked the Lord for it. For only in Jesus is there true reconciliation and harmony.

What, then, did this Pretoria crusade demonstrate to South Africa, sick with prejudice and weeping because of the human damage caused by apartheid?

Simply this: if South Africa is truly a Christian nation then it needs to turn Godward for its solutions. The Christianity of the nation has been mostly lip service. Its past style of Christianity has been stained with the bile of racism and the time is now come for White leaders to hear and do the Word of God. Psalm 82 surely speaks to South Africa and all its leaders:

"How long will ye judge unjustly, and accept persons of the wicked? Defend the poor and fatherless: do justice to the afflicted and needy. Deliver the poor and needy: rid them out of the hand of the wicked." (Psalm 82v2-4 KJV).

The answer is: do it God's way. To reject the way of peace offered by practical Christianity will bring South Africa into perilous and dark times.

The answers, not only to the South African problem, but to all of mankind, were encapsulated in that Pretoria crusade in 1985. It was a different crusade. It lacked the spontaneity of Ibadan, the zest of Harare, but it was a crusade characterised by waves of divine love, that reached down into the depths of every heart. If only it could be repeated on a bigger and grander scale right through the nation.

This great victory for love and unity was forged by long and arduous planning by the Pretoria Crusade committee, on which men like Pastor Willie Crew laboured with a large and enthusiastic team of volunteers. They worked for months, ensuring that the event would go off smoothly.

There was also the spiritual preparation and warfare, spearheaded, of course, by Suzette Hattingh. Few of the city's population knew anything about it. It was almost an invisible battle, except for a hardy band of 500 intercessory prayer soldiers, who raised their voices to heaven and released the power of God over the city.

"When I arrived in Pretoria to prepare the intercessory prayer squads I immediately sensed a strong spiritual resistance," recalls Suzette.

Realising that they were in for a battle Suzette soon got rid of the slackness in the volunteers' prayer lives. "I knew I had to teach them how to make war and that God was raising up an army for himself," she added.

And from then on it was all-out warfare - in the spirit realm as night after night from 300 to 500 people (of all races) gathered to listen to the Word and to intercede.

"It was the highest level of unity in spiritual warfare that I have ever experienced in our crusades. Not only were we interceding for the crusade, but for the city as well. People began to stand in authority and pray with a deep assurance that their prayers were turning back the enemy. They knew they were engaged in real spiritual combat," she said.

This accent on warfare was in contrast to the spirit of travail that characterised the 1984 crusade in Harare. "On that occasion there was a deep cry in Harare for the nation. In Pretoria it was confrontation with the powers of darkness," explains Suzette.

Suzette directs her intercessors like a general. On the final Saturday night and Sunday afternoon the intercessors changed strategy and instead of remaining in a hall at the back of the stadium, they moved in among the crowd.

"We had people under the platform, praying all the time and other intercessors ringed the front of the platform. We built up a 'wall' of prayer. Other groups were in the grandstand."

The impact of Suzette's rather special ministry not only produces glorious results during the CFAN crusades, but is having a profound effect on those who engage in this type of praying. They hardly ever remain the same again and go back to their churches, on fire and thrilled to have got to grips with the reality of prayer. Many pastors have been inspired by this often revolutionary approach to prayer. At the start some pastors regarded the intercessory group as "just another prayer meeting". This attitude soon changed once they became absorbed in the teaching and practise of genuine intercession.

Besides the wonderful love and joy that marked this crusade there were also some warming testimonies, like that given by a young Hindu man, who could hardly contain the thrill and joy of finding Jesus as his Saviour. He explained how he had come forward to receive Jesus as His personal Saviour and at that precise moment he had felt the darkness of satanic bondage leave him.

"I knew I had been delivered from the devil," he told the listening audience. And when he returned to his home that night he received another surprise. His younger brother met him at the door with an eager question: was he a Christian? And then the young man realised that his younger brother had secretly given his heart to Jesus and was saved too!

Co-evangelist Michael Kolisang led the prayers for the sick night after night as he, Reinhard and other pastors ministered to the long lines of sick, lame, and blind people who waited patiently in the wintery night air.

On the final Friday night the faith of the crowd was ignited when a woman, brought to the stadium in an ambulance, walked through the crowd, testifying that she had been touched by the Lord. She was Mrs Aletta Wolmarans, of Gezina, who was seriously injured in a motor accident 16 years ago. After Kolisang prayed for her, she insisted on getting off the ambulance stretcher and walking up and down in front of the platform. Later, she climbed up the ramp to the stage and gave thanks to the Lord when Reinhard asked her to tell the crowd what had happened to her.

The ambulance attendants both testified that Mrs Wolmarans had been almost helpless before coming to the meeting and her local pastor confirmed that she had been ill for a long while and that since being prayed for her condition was improving.

On the same night a teenage girl, squint in both eyes for 13 years, left the meeting healed. Friends confirmed that the girl's eye condition had been dramatically improved.

Dozens more claimed healing, for hearing conditions, eyesight and for various other diseases, testimony to the Word of God which declares: *"I am the Lord that healeth thee."* (Psalm 103 verse 3). But the greatest joy of all was expressed for the 5,300 decisions that were registered during the crusade and who were closely followed up by the dozens of churches which co-operated to make this such a wonderful crusade.

Chapter 7

Return to Zambia

ONE of the frequent questions that prayer partners and supporters of CFAN ask is: what is a crusade in Africa really like? What goes on - behind the scenes? What is life like during a crusade? What do the CFAN team do?

These are valid enquiries because few of Reinhard's dear and much treasured prayer partners ever get the opportunity to experience the innermost workings of a big crusade in Africa. Even those few, from Germany, Britain, or the USA, who have made the trip to Africa, don't always get into the nitty-gritty of crusade life.

In August-September 1985 I flew to Lusaka to report on the closing four days of the crusade in the capital city of Zambia and then travelled by road with the CFAN team to Lubumbashi, in southern Zaire, during which time I lived, ate, laughed and cried with the CFAN team. The following chapters are written deliberately from a personal viewpoint, so as to convey to the reader the red-raw facts of crusading for Jesus in Africa.

There was a tingle behind the back of my neck when I stepped onto the tarmac of Lusaka international airport on Wednesday, August 21, 1985. I had returned to the land of my spiritual birth. Yes, in May 1961 - 24 years previously - I had accepted Jesus Christ as my Saviour in Faith Tabernacle in the copper-mining town of Mufulira. Then in December 1964 I had answered the call of God to the ministry and had come to Lusaka where I had pastored at Calvary Tabernacle for nearly three years. Since then I'd left preaching to go back into newspapers, until joining Christ For All Nations as their fulltime editor and publicist in 1982. With me now was our photographer Tony Fredriksson. We were met at the airport by Kobus de Lange.

The Lusaka crusade had already been in progress for ten days when we arrived. The meetings had been planned for the evening, but because of security restrictions the crusade was being held during daylight hours. This meant starting at two o'clock each afternoon.

When we got to Matero sports field at 1.30 pm the first people had already taken up the first 15 rows of benches. Despite the awkward hour, it seemed that many thousands of people in Lusaka were somehow taking time off work in the afternoon to get to the crusade. By two o'clock there was a steady stream of people flowing into the grounds - and two hours later they were still arriving, even though Reinhard was almost halfway through preaching.

This is one idiosyncrasy of Africa - time stands still for most people. Deadlines and the chase to keep up with the clock are the pursuits of westerners. Watches are not really regarded as time pieces, but as jewellery!

Reinhard preached a typical, powerful gospel message, and almost from the moment he opened his mouth to speak, there were outbursts of screaming from people in the crowd as demonic powers manifested themselves. These demon manifestations,

I was told, had marked the crusade right from its first day, and they continued until the final Saturday.

Suddenly a woman would fall over backwards or leap up and start wailing and writhing, as an evil power manifested itself. Ushers would rush in to get the person out and it would often take up to four grown men to carry one demon-possessed women to a cordoned-off area next to the platform.

Here the person would be laid on the grass while counsellors prayed for them. Again tremendous violence was displayed by these people as Christians attempted to cast out the evil spirits. It was a common sight to see a counsellor sitting bodily on top of a victim's legs, while two further counsellors held down the person's arms and prayed for them. The victims would still twist and buck, tossing their heads from side to side and contorting their faces in gruesome gestures. Sometimes the eyes were totally glazed. Or sometimes they were wild, and defiant, as though Satan himself were taunting the counsellors. Significantly 99 per cent of these "victims" were women.

This was so because the influence of witchcraft is still very common, even in the capital of Lusaka. Instead of consulting a qualified medical practitioner, the women invariably go to a witchdoctor for any personal illness or when a child gets sick. Marriage problems also result in visits to the witchdoctor.

The menfolk, who work in the towns and city, tend to give more credence to conventional medical care, but make little or no attempt to stop their women from going to witchdoctors. Thus the high incidence of demonic activity among the women who came to the meetings. Many were set free and encouraged to burn the fetishes and throw away the potions they had obtained, but many found it hard to believe that Jesus Christ could deliver them and keep them free from evil spirits. Because of this strong witchdoctor influence on women, the young children are also brought up in the aura of witchcraft which, coupled with worship of ancestral spirits, is still a powerful force that binds millions of people in Africa.

Despite these interruptions the crowd of 15,000 listened appreciatively to the gospel and after the altar call Reinhard and Michael Kolisang began to pray for the sick. The press of people wanting to be prayed for became so great that Reinhard could not cope with the rush. It is in moments like this that the CFAN team come into action, not only controlling the crowd, but by also actively getting involved in ministry. So desperate and so ill are many people that they are more than satisfied to have any CFAN person pray for them.

On that Wednesday afternoon, with the sun fading fast and a chill wind frisking at my jacket, I pushed my way into the crowd. It is in these situations that one discovers just how great the needs are.

A woman pushed forward her young son, about four years old. His body was grotesquely twisted and deformed. Pleading eyes searched my face. I prayed for the young boy, but I had hardly finished when another woman shoved in front of me with a tiny baby. In the space of five minutes I must have prayed for 20 people and still the pushing didn't stop.

I gazed up and saw that Reinhard, Michael, Kenneth Meshoe, Kobus de Lange and others of the team were all faced with queues of people wanting to be prayed for.

Reinhard, his voice now hoarse and dry from preaching and praying, saw a break in the crowd and bolted off for the CFAN camp which consisted of a laager of the trucks and trailers arranged on an adjacent field.

An insistent pulling at my jacket sleeve brought me back to the need to keep praying for a line of people. Young and old, all with that same despairing look in their eyes, reached out for a touch from Jesus. Many could not speak English so I did not even know what to pray for, but prayed.

The crowd began to thin out when a short, thick set young man of about 20 stood in front of me. A ragged coat covered a yellowy, discoloured shirt. From a casual glance he looked fit and well. I leaned forward and asked what was wrong with him? In halting English he said:

"My heart, a bad heart..." and put his hand over his chest. I took a step closer, put one hand on his shoulder and placed my right hand over his heart. I almost pulled my hand away, so startling was the pounding within this young man's chest. It felt as though his heart was in a wild spasm and would come careering out of his chest! Tears welled in my eyes, compassion washed over me. Here was a youth in the prime of life, but even my unskilled knowledge of medical science told me that unless some miracle occurred, this young man would not live to see old age. I prayed and then walked away across the floodlit grass of Matero football field. People still wandered around.

People still wanted you to pray for them. In fact, I could have stayed there until midnight, but there's a limit to what my emotions can stand. The helplessness of the sick, especially the young, and the effort of praying, in earnest, left me tired and drained.

I joined my colleagues in the kitchen cum dining

room. It's a giant steel container with the kitchen (gas stove, sink etc) at one end with wooden tables on tressles and wooden planks running along each side for seating. About 30 plus can be seated at one sitting. I enjoyed a couple of slices of bread and jam and two cups of coffee. (The main meal during crusades is served at mid-day).

The next question was where would Tony and I be sleeping? Kobus told us we had been billeted with two of our musicians, Tommy Saaiden and Trevor Sampson, who were staying in the house of a Zambian airline pilot, Jasper Chibolela. Somehow we commandeered some transport and were soon being welcomed by our Zambian hosts and Tony and myself were shown to a bedroom which we were to share. It had been a long and strenuous day, and it was close to 11 o'clock before we got to lay our heads down.

Next morning, after a delightful breakfast prepared by our charming host, the four of us - Tommy, Trevor, Tony and myself - joined the rest of the CFAN team at a local church across town for a time of prayer and intercession for the afternoon's meeting.

From there I paid a brief visit to Calvary Tabernacle, off Great East Road, the church I had once pastored. It had been extended and several new outbuildings filled the ground. In fact, the offices of the church had become the headquarters for the CFAN organising staff for the Lusaka crusade. I was thrilled to learn that the church was thriving and filled to capacity on Sundays.

After leaving the four of us decided to pay a visit to one of the local markets - to get some photographs and see for ourselves what was available in the foodline.

Markets in Africa are mostly the same - smelly, full of flies and rather unhygienic. Open sewers wind between mud and grass structures with dingy interiors and crooked wooden shelves on which a pathetic few tins of tobacco, stale looking sweets or bundles of candles are precariously balanced. This market place in Lusaka is not a tourist attraction and our presence was not welcomed. Within a few minutes of arriving and taking a few casual photographs we were harangued by some self-appointed market marshals, who insisted on destroying our film and hustling us out of the market.

I suppose we could have objected and created a scene, but decided that it was not worth the trouble and we did not want to prejudice the reason for being in Lusaka, which was to win people to Jesus. From the market we drove to the Matero grounds to have lunch and to witness what the Lord was going to do that afternoon.

Again the crowd was in the region of 15,000 and again the outbursts of demonic-inspired women echoed through the crowd. In fact, it had become so much a part of the service that Reinhard was hardly perturbed by the rushing of ushers into the crowd to get to another "possessed" person. Even the crowd was calm, hanging on to every word, somehow sensing that today they would find the truth to set them free of all this satanic influence which was patently a part of daily life.

Before preaching, Reinhard read out some stirring testimonies which he had received from people during the past few days of the crusade. They were inspirational, uplifting the audience and setting the tone for another rousing meeting.

One remarkable story came from a young man who had been healed while waiting at a bus stop outside the stadium! He suffered from a severe form of athritis in his legs and could only hobble along. While standing at the bus stop a half mile away from the stadium he heard Reinhard saying: "Lift up your hands and receive your healing." And he did!

A grandmother, Mrs Rebecca Mwandela, from Pika, travelled several hundred miles to get to the crusade. She had great difficulty walking and brought her sick grandchild as well. After a mass prayer for the sick by co-evangelist Michael Kolisang, they were both healed.

On Friday morning we again gathered in the "borrowed" church to pray and share the Word together. On this morning, Pastor Adam Mtsweni, long-time crusade song leader, opened his heart to his colleagues. Because he was South African-born he realised that he could not go very much further into Africa and so he had decided to leave and start a church of his own back home. There was a sadness, but there was no solution yet, for South Africans to travel freely into Africa because of the ongoing political struggle in RSA.

A special treat beckoned us on arrival at the CFAN camp. Marcel Allegrucci, a professional chef, who at one time almost joined the team, but who is now working with another ministry, was preparing lunch. From the rather drab interior of the cream-painted container, came the sizzling sound of steak and the aroma of garlic. If you closed your eyes you could have transported yourself into a five-star restaurant!

Friday afternoon was advertised as "Holy Spirit Day". Reinhard always sets aside one service at which to preach on the baptism of the Spirit and this was to be the afternoon. Almost 20,000 people filled the ground and when the time came a mass of people came forward, eager to receive "power from on high".

Tony Fredriksson decided to get a different angle for his photograph of the occasion and I helped him place a ladder on the edge of the huge crowd. We thought we were on the edge, but by the time Kolisang began to pray for a mass baptism of the Holy Spirit, we realised we were completely surrounded. A great "hallelujah" ripped skywards and then, in three separate waves, the people began to fall to the ground. One of these waves came rolling directly towards the ladder on which Tony was perched and which I was trying to keep balanced for him.

Fortunately some ushers saw our predicament and the falling bodies were somehow steered clear of our ladder.

These mass baptisms in the Spirit are always fascinating. Cynics say that it's impossible to tell whether a person is truly speaking in another tongue because it is probably their own native dialect. True. But if you've been around in Pentecost for a few years, your ear becomes receptive to heavenly languages and many "tongues" do sound similar and as I picked myself through the crowd there were a multitude of new tongue-talkers around me! As I turned to see how Tony and his ladder were doing I saw a woman lying prostrate on the ground, her handbag clutched to her chest, grass in her hair, and a beam of joy on her face. It was Anne, our host's wife. She had just been baptised in the Holy Ghost.

The meeting closed, but for some hours afterwards there were scores of people still wandering across the field, praising the Lord and praying for one another. The power of the mighty Spirit of God had been poured out in great measure that afternoon. Now all attention was on the closing Saturday afternoon service.

A big crowd was expected and we were not disappointed. As I clamoured up the iron steps to the kitchen container, I looked out over the low-lying offices and changerooms of the stadium and saw a long line of people straggling toward the grounds and it was only one o'clock. By three o'clock the field was a sea of people, with an estimated 40,000 people singing and praising God.

The meeting officially started at two o'clock with singing and then a choir sang. CFAN soloist Tommy Saaiden sang two items and then a series of thanks dragged on the meeting and when Reinhard came to preach the gospel I remember looking at my watch -it was 4.20 pm!

A Zambia television crew arrived on the last day to shoot film for a documentary on CFAN. Heading the ZTV crew was Mr Chewe Chiluba, who accepted Jesus when CFAN were in Lusaka in 1981. It was a thrill to speak to him and to know that, indeed, the fruit of that year is still flourishing. In fact, throughout the crusade people came up to us and expressed delight that we had returned. Many had their first encounter with Jesus in the old CFAN Yellow Tent which had been pitched in the self same Matero stadium four years earlier. To hear these reports is always rewarding, like when Reinhard arrived at Lusaka airport, the official checking his passport smiled with delight and told him: "I've got a sermon tape of yours".

Earlier in the crusade when Reinhard was invited

to appear on Zambia Television, he was met by a journalist who said: "Four years ago I found Christ as Saviour under your ministry. So did my wife. At that time my wife suffered from terrible abscesses and no doctor could help her. When she received Jesus in the Yellow Tent the abscesses dried up and have gone to this day!"

The altar call on the final Saturday afternoon netted another wonderful harvest, although by the end of the day the grounds looked something like a battlefield as the number of demon-possessed people had been larger than usual and the screaming, moaning writhing bodies had been deposited at various places around the grounds. Long after the meeting had finished devoted counsellors were still praying and casting out evil spirits in the ongoing spiritual battle that is unseen, yet is ever present with all on this earth.

That night we relaxed with Jasper and his wife and children, watching some television before turning in for a good night's rest. I had to be up at 5.00 am to get to the CFAN site for breakfast and then leave with the truck convoy for Zaire. Little did I know then that this would be my last night of good, sound sleep in a proper bed. It would be nine days before I would feel the comfort of an innersprung mattress, or enjoy a hot bath!

The sun was hardly up when I arrived at the camp site and after a good breakfast I watched the men pack away and load the last few items, including the water purification plant. I was later to regret I hadn't taken a keener interest in this, because it fell on me to pull it apart when we left Lubumbashi!

I got some further last minute hints on how to work the CFAN camera from Tony, who was returning by air to South Africa. I was also to act as our official photographer for the Zaire crusade.

After what seemed an age the trailers were hitched and the huge left-hand drive Mecurius Deutz motors roared and the convoy started sorting itself out. I hitched a ride with our transport manager Don Preen, who was driving one of the heaviest-laden of the trucks. The particular trailer we were pulling carried the heavy crusade platform, the steel poles and masts which bear the floodlights. As the vehicles edged across the sports field, kicking up dry, brown grass and clouds of dust it seemed a pity to be leaving so soon because the response of the Zambian people to the gospel had been so wonderful and so joyful that one felt we could stay on for ever and preach there. But the task of caring and carrying on the gospel thrust was now left in the hands of the local churches. They shouldered this responsibility now.

As the long CFAN convoy of vehicles pulled out of Matero stadium, hundreds of Christians lined the roadside to bless and cheer the team as it pushed on to Zaire, to challenge another stronghold of Satan.

When the convoy steered out onto the Great North Road, it consisted of one minibus, three small closed trucks, three caravans, one motor car and five beautiful red and white painted trucks. It was a colourful and impressive convoy that pulled up over the hill. One of those trucks would never return. Nor the men, who were now happily chatting together in the cab, looking forward to the crusade in Lubumbashi.

I looked at my watch as Don geared up the truck. It was 9 o'clock on a beautiful, sunny Sunday morning. Ahead of us lay a drive of 260 miles and it was calculated we would reach the town of Chingola by nightfall. We would stay there overnight and leave early on Monday morning for the Zambia-Zaire border, only 42 miles further on. Once clear of the border we hoped to be in the city of Lubumbashi by lunchtime on Monday.

It was a new experience driving in a massive long-haulage truck, especially a left-hand drive vehicle. I soon realised I was the "eyes" for driver Don when it came to overtaking slower-moving traffic. It wasn't that easy; in fact a bit hazardous trying to calculate on-coming speeds and just how much time and space we needed to get our horse and 30-foot trailer past another moving vehicle. Fortunately Don, a short, stocky man in his late forties, has no pretensions to being a Nigel Mansell or Alain Prost when he's behind the wheel and we struck up a good bit of teamwork, piloting our giant rig along the highways and some of the tiny byways of the towns we went through. I'll still never know how we didn't take a set of traffic lights with us when we cut a corner a little shallow in the town of Ndola later that afternoon!

It was a good trip, although slow, because of the police road checks which one encounters on the roads in Zambia. This is because of smuggling of hard-to-get foodstuffs (mainly luxury items) and, of course, drugs. Zambia, unfortunately, is a dropping off point for a major drug-pedalling ring which operates between India, Zambia and South Africa.

Our convoy pulled into Chingola at 5 o'clock and parked on a sandy, vacant lot just off the main street. In fact, we were parked almost in the middle of the main shopping area!

Chingola is a copper mining town with the nearby Nchanga mines the richest ore-bearing copper mines in the world. Our convoy formed a rough square and we then took stock of the position. A quick stroll the length and breadth of the main street revealed no public toilets and certainly nothing resembling a shower. Fortunately, a local pastor arrived and took the three women in our party - Isabelle de Lange, Val Kasselman and Shireen West - back to his home for a hot bath. For the 17 remaining men, there was going to be no hot shower and not even a washbasin. After being awake from 5 o'clock in the morning and travelling all day I was almost prepared to pawn my birthright for the luxury of a warm, soapy bath. But it was not to be - but at least we had food!

Later, when the women folk returned, they found a roaring fire going and the men cooking some giant T-bone steaks on the open flames. We sat under the open, starry sky, barbecuing - right in the middle of the town, with curious looks coming from window shoppers. Having satisfied our hunger, the next thing was to wash.

Fortunately we found a tap (cold water) in one corner of the vacant lot. So, armed with soap, towel, toothpaste and toothbrush I set off for the tap. It wasn't an ordinary tap because it was set in the ground at ankle level, with a dubiously dark drain underneath it. Tall grass grew vigorously around the tap.

For a person who has spent most of his life in the city and used to chrome and tiled bathrooms this was really living it rough. Little did I know what lay ahead in the next 24 hours. Anyway, I smiled to myself as I brushed my teeth in Kwacha Avenue. I was sure not many residents of the town had ever done that. I certainly wasn't going to make a habit of it!

My thoughts now turned to sleep, or rather my

eyelids informed me that they had been open for a good 16 hours and that we were due to be on the road again by 8 o'clock the next morning.

One of the steel containers had been converted into a communal dormitory with two-tier steel bunkbeds in it and a few austere steel hanging cupboards.

I was pointed to a top bunk and quickly changed into pyjamas, then hoisted myself up. But not before it had been decided that guard duty should be done during the night by all those who hadn't been driving. I magnanimously volunteered to do the dogwatch from 4.00 am to 6.00 am. I figured on getting to sleep promptly and the thought of rising early was not that daunting. What I didn't take into account was the fact that in our sleeping container were four people who were going to be sharing the two-hour security shifts.

I was in bed by 11 o'clock. I soon found that besides being a very hard bunk, the paper thin mattress rustled and crackled loudly each time I turned. Also on a top bunk at my feet was Chris Alberts, one of our crusade organisers, who had started up the most wicked snoring. Then an icy draught started blowing on me from a tiny fanlight above my bed - and I couldn't shut it.

At midnight the first shift came off. Basil Erasmus came up the ladder to the container, pushing open the steel door, which creaked and groaned and then, with a metallic "clung" closed. I discovered Basil was my sleeping partner on the lower bunk. Everytime he turned I felt as though the bunk was tipping over. Added to this was the fact that each time Kim Fullam turned in the driver's bunk in his cab which was still hooked up to the trailer, the whole container swayed as though in a heaving Atlantic swell!

Sleep was not going to come easy, but I determinedly shut my eyes and tried to doze off. Just as I began to get drowsy it was the end of the next two-hour shift and the steel door creaked open and clanged shut. Then there was a commotion trying to get Albert Hartnick out of bed and on duty. I just lay there and did the only useful thing I could do - I prayed. I was scheduled to go on duty at 4.00 am, but at about 3.30 am I decided to get up and tell Kevin Royston that I would take over the rest of his shift.

It was extremely cool as I paced around the shadowy outline of our fleet of vehicles. We had several guard dogs with us, which were tied up on free-running chains at two ends of the camp. It suddenly occurred to me that the dogs didn't know me as well as they knew the rest of the Team and that they might mistake me for an intruder, especially as I was wrapped up and brandished a heavy wooden stick! I decided to give the dogs a wide berth as I patrolled the outer perimeter of the camp. I need not have worried - the dogs were fast asleep. I wondered who was guarding whom?

As the first tinges of red stained the sky I wondered just how I was going to survive the day. I had not slept for over 24 hours, but consoled myself with the fact that our destination of Lubumbashi was only 135 miles away and that we would be there within a few short hours. Little did I realise just what a long and harrowing day lay ahead. Still, the joy of the Lord was in my heart and that meant that He would strengthen me. And He did.

After a breakfast of hot porridge and a slice or two of bread (no toast available), the kitchen container was made secure and by 7 o'clock the convoy wound its way through the early morning traffic of Chingola and out onto the main road, heading for the Zaire border.

We had only travelled for about 15 minutes when the convoy halted on the side of the road. Because of the lack of ablution facilities in the town, it had been impossible to go anywhere and now, with plenty of open bush available, some of the men had to obey an urgent call of nature. So with toilet rolls fluttering in the wind, several of the team dashed for the cover of the tall grass!

We were soon moving again, but after only a short while were halted. This time a police road block. A quick explanation of who we were and we were cheerily waved on and soon by-passed Chililila-bombwe, the last town before the border post. The road became narrower, but it was still in good condition and we began to make speed, knowing that the border was only a few miles ahead. With the border post in sight, we were stopped at another road block, this one heavily armed with a sinsister-looking machine gun emplacement just off the side of the road - a stern warning to anyone who tried to make a wild dash for the border. There were no hitches at the checkpoint and we pulled off again and reached the border at 9.30 am. It had taken us two and a half hours to cover the 42 miles.

We were swiftly cleared at the Zambian post and passed through to the Zaire side where we were met by Pastor Ronald Monat, a missionary in that country all his life and CFAN's key man in putting together the Lubumbashi crusade. He had travelled to the border so as to assist with interpretation because very little English is spoken in Zaire. The main languages are French and Swahili.

Chapter 8

Miracles in Lubumbashi

THE sight of our convoy parked at the border post soon attracted a flock of young children who had to be restrained from poring all over our vehicles. They took a special delight in teasing our guard dogs, who travelled in a special steel-netted cage on the back of one of the small trucks. It grew hotter and stickier as we milled around, waiting to have our passports stamped and for the multiple pieces of paper to be cleared by customs. I longed to reach Lubumbashi where the prospect of a hot bath or shower and a bed were all that really interested me.

It was over two hours before the boom was raised and we officially crossed into Zaire. The trucks had hardly moved out of low gear when we came to another police checkpoint and Ronald Monat, who was leading the convoy to the city, had to get out and give a long explanation of who we were and what we were going to do in Lubumbashi. Meanwhile, the sun baked down and the cab of the truck became almost unbearable. All I wanted to do was sleep.

Just after 2.30 pm we entered Lubumbashi, a city which in the early 1960s had made world headlines, when as the Belgian-named Elizabethville, it had been the stronghold of the cessessionist leader Moise Tshombe, who had employed a private army of mercenaries to help him in his attempt to gain independence for the province of Katanga.

It was once a cosmopolitan city, well patronised by the rich White miners from neighbouring Zambia (then Northern Rhodesia), who found the nightclubs and gambling dens a great attraction. When Belgium granted independence and pulled out - almost overnight - the nation was plunged into chaos and anarchy and a ruthless struggle developed for control of the country. Some of the worst fighting and gravest atrocities happened in and around Elizabethville.

Now, as we drove through the city, 25 years after Zaire gained its independence, I was amazed to see some stark reminders of that bloody civil war. Some buildings, burnt out during the fighting still stood, desolate black shells. A mile long brick wall was still pock-marked with bullet holes, and behind it walls of some of the buildings were also scarred. But these silent memorials to death and destruction were not the things which made a first impression on me.

Two things hit me, and remain imprinted on my mind - the swamp green coloured taxis and the hordes of children. It was like a circus coming to town, as hundreds of children ran and danced along the pavement as our long convoy edged through the streets.

We headed first for the central customs and immigration offices where some more formalities and papers had to be checked and while we sat in our parked vehicles I began to wonder whether maybe I was hallucinating because of the lack of sleep. The pavement next to my side of the cab was just a continuous drove of passing children, who were also very adept at pickpocketing and at snatching any item left unguarded as our sound man, Roger West found out. He had a jersey across the back of his seat and in a brief moment when his back was turned a little hand flashed through the open window and whipped it out. By the time Roger had opened his door to give chase the child thief had vanished.

Bleary-eyed I looked at Don, who remarked, also rather cautiously: "There seem to be a lot of children around here." Well, I was pleased I wasn't imagining it, but it turned out that it was school holidays, plus the birth rate over the past few years has rocketed. Children make up more than 35 per cent of the 750,000 population of Lubumbashi.

The other lasting impression was the small, minibus taxis which bumped and bounced around every street and corner, carrying the most unbelievable number of people. When we finished with the customs formalities our convoy headed for the President Mobuto stadium, which was to be the venue for the crusade.

As we carefully manoeuvred down the main street, these bustling taxis threaded past us. Most of them were at least 15 years old and most looked like they belonged on a scrapheap. In fact the road often looked like a moving scrapyard of green metal! Windscreens were cracked, fenders buckled or non-existent, and every one had some welding on the bodywork. Inside these normal six to seven seaters, were sandwiched 10 or 12 adults - and their baggage, which was sometimes a live chicken! One taxi bounced past us - shock absorbers long since worn out - and hanging halfway out of the side door was a passenger, quite content to know that he was riding home and not walking.

The tall towers of the banked floodlights of the stadium came into view and after some twisting and turning we passed through some rusty old corrugated iron gates and into the sports grounds. On the right was the stadium, ringed by an embankment of concrete seats and a steep covered grandstand, under which were situated offices and changerooms. The thought of a shower immediately came to mind as we drove past this block.

Our vehicles laagered on an adjacent practice sportsfield and the men began their next task of setting up a proper liveable camp for the next seven days.

The stadium where we were situated was in the middle of a residential area, and opposite a large open-air market, so that, despite the lateness of the afternoon there were still a lot of people around, especially children, who spent a large part of their days playing football on the fields that we were parked on. Within half an hour of our arrival we were surrounded by a thousand or more young children, who unmercifully taunted the guard dogs and threatened to overrun our camp - if given the opportunity!

We were all exhausted and haggard from a long and tedious day of stop-go driving, so that the presence of the children and the loud chattering and giggling began to touch a few raw nerves.

Of first concern was to walk across the field to the back of the grandstand and inspect what ablution facilities were available. As was to be expected there were plenty of cloakroom facilities for the public and so it seemed that at least one basic need was going to be met. When I drew near an awful stench reached my nostrils. I walked into the first toilet block and recoiled in disgust. Don, who was with me, ventured into a block further along, and came out holding a handkerchief to his mouth and gasped: "Don't go in there, you'll be sick." I passed by that one and went into another public convenience on the far corner of the grandstand. I entered and immediately stepped into something soft and sticky and then my stomach turned as I hastily retreated. The state of the place was unbelievable. Urine and human excretion plastered toilets, washbasins, floors and walls. It would take weeks to clean the place. But there was still hope.

We found the main gates to the offices and team changerooms under the grandstand were securely locked, so that there was every chance that these facilities were clean, especially as an international football match against Kenya was planned for the Sunday after we left.

Meanwhile, the hordes of children were becoming more hostile towards us and it was decided to let the dogs loose. Danie Kasselman, who had charge of the dogs, was sure he would be able to call them back before they attacked and bit anyone. When the children saw we were in earnest about letting the dogs off their leads they turned and fled, with the young alsatians in hot pursuit. On command they returned to Danie, but so did the children. It now became a game as to just how far they could encroach on our camp before we set the dogs on them.

In the middle of all this chaos one local Christian brother tried to make his way through the throng of children to welcome us to Lubumbashi. Unfortunately, he got caught in the middle of a dog charge and was nipped on his leg. One of our drivers, Gerry Davies, had to run to his rescue.

To add to the tension, Danie's young son, Leon fell badly while trying to help with some unloading and badly wrenched his knee. I was called to come and pray for him and to calm nerves which were reaching breaking point, even among the team.

Besides the children on the field, the 12-foot high wall near to which we were parked, was now ringed with hundreds of children, their legs dangling over the wall as they kept up incessant commentary - in French and Swahili.

The frustration of not being able to communicate with the children aggravated matters. Anyway, the sun was fast fading and we hoped that with nightfall the children would disperse and leave us in peace. My concern, though, was to get into the changerooms under the stadium.

Eventually we found a key and I entered. My first disappointment was to find that there was no electric light - all the bulbs had been stolen out of their sockets. I stepped into the changerooms. A sickly smell hit my stomach. The water had been turned off and the toilets and urinal hadn't been flushed for weeks. They were filthy, but not as bad as those outside.

Next I went to the showers. I pushed open a door - and shut it smartly. It, too, had been used as a toilet. Also a swarm of mosquitoes descended on my head and face. I looked up at the ceiling and at the door of the next shower; it was covered black with mosquitoes. The changerooms were a huge incubator for thousands of mosquitoes.

Of the ten showers I checked, only two were useable, but they needed to be scrubbed. The once white tiles were rusty cream and flecked with dried, soapy dirt. Dead insects, a squashed frog and other unidentifiable grime covered the floor.

I commandeered two local men who indicated they worked in the stadium. Unable to speak the language I used sufficient sign language to get them to bring buckets and a hose pipe. I ran back to the camp to get scrubbing brushes, soap and as much disinfectant as I could lay my hands on.

The rest of the team were busy unloading and so I found that I was now the self-appointed health officer in charge of toilets and showers.

I amazed myself because I have no stomach for such things. I grabbed the hose pipe and proceeded to flood the changerooms, while telling my two labourers to sweep out the water. It was the dirtiest job I have ever done and probably will ever do. But I was motivated. I dearly wanted to have a warm shower and get clean myself.

Next I tackled the two showers which I had earmarked for our use. I scrubbed the tiles, almost blew my sinuses out from the heavy ammonia fumes from the cleaning liquid I was pouring everywhere. When I turned on the showers, I discovered, to my great disappointment, that there was no hot water, only icy cold. Still, I was sure our electrician Milton would remedy things the next day.

It was dark by the time I'd finished cleaning out the changerooms, but I was confident that they were now useable and well disinfected. Now to try them out! I'm no lover of cold showers but after living for two days in the same clothes and no bath, it was a breath of heaven to smell the freshness of soap and water on my skin again. I was beginning to get a peep into crusade life in Africa!

After a good dinner, came another shock. Guard duty! I was no hero this time. I volunteered for the first stint from 9.00 pm to 11.00 pm. I also protested about sleeping in the creaking, clunging, swaying container and Don offered to share the cab of his truck with me. Home, for the next seven days, was going to be a truck cab!

With one of the alsatians on a lead I did a tour of the camp, which was well lit up, as we had our own generator. Although we had managed to lock the gate and keep the children out of the ground they still lined the high wall overlooking us. A few stones and large rocks had been hurled at us earlier by a few troublemakers, but fortunately no damage was done. As I patrolled a new word, which would ring in all of our ears each day, came from the children on the wall: "Hey, meester, meester," taunting us good-naturedly - most of the time.

I finished my guard-duty in a sleep walk, because little is recalled after my head hit my pillow in the sardine-can-like bunk of my new bedroom in Don's truck. Sleep had never been so welcomed.

The next morning, Tuesday, we decided it was impossible to have the CFAN camp sited in its present position because of the security risk posed by the children, especially when the camp was not occupied, which would happen while the meetings were on. So it was decided that the best and most secure spot for the camp would be inside the main stadium at the back of the one set of goal posts.

The entire arena was ringed by a high barbed-wire fence, which would keep out intruders. Kobus anticipated that Reinhard would be unhappy about having the camp in the middle of the stadium, but the advantages outweighed the censure he might incur from Reinhard. And so the trucks, trailers and caravans were moved and the next major task was to get the lighting, sound system and platform rigged. The first meeting was scheduled for 3 o'clock the next afternoon.

Local churches provided plenty of labour to help our team with their tough manual jobs, but the language barrier was again an obstacle, as the Tech Team tried desperately to tell the local helpers what tools to use and what materials were needed. It was also a searingly hot day with a blustery wind, kicking up dust and dry grass all through the day. My blue jeans were a pale shade of brown by evening and my hair had changed to a reddish brown colour.

The children were back, from just after breakfast, but this time a barbed-wire fence kept them at bay, although there were quite a few who dared to climb over the fence, possibly lured on by our washing which was strung out on makeshift lines tied between the kitchen container and one of the caravans. This, in fact, became a daily challenge. Several local Christian women came each day to do our washing in big iron tubs out in the open and the temptation of our shirts, jeans and shorts hanging on the line was just too much for some of the youngsters, who braved the barbed wire and the guard dogs to attempt a quick snatch. But we managed to protect our clothing for the whole week and as far as I know never had anything valuable stolen.

Towards mid-day the number of children on the stands must have been about 5,000 at least and this was to remain the norm for the rest of our stay there. They stared and called "meester, meester", all day. The noise of their shouting, cheering and taunting was almost like that of a crowd at a football match.

As I walked under the shadow of the giant concrete grandstand, I couldn't help reflecting on the old Roman coliseum, with the Christians in the arena and their tormentors sitting, gloating in the stands. But it wasn't a defeatist thought, because we were here to feed the roaring lion that is Satan to the Christians! Of that I was confident.

During the course of the day Milton tried, in vain, to find some means of getting us hot water for our showers, but at the end of a hot, windy and grubby day a cold shower was welcome. Earlier I had declared war on the mosquitoes in the changerooms - and almost suffocated myself by emptying several cans of insect spray.

Later that evening we had an unfortunate incident with some of the unruly element among the children, who, besides taunting the dogs, also threw stones at some of the team. Some of the team chased the offenders and one youngster got the shock of his life when he found himself over someone's knee, his bottom well and truly tanned! The incident caused some strife within the team when somebody pointed out that we were here to show the love of God and preach the gospel and not beat up children! After some open debate and prayer the differences were resolved and the incident buried. A new guard duty roster was organised and to my delight I was no longer included. In fact, now that the camp was behind the wire we were able to let the dogs run loose at night.

After brushing my teeth by the side of the plastic water tank fitted on my truck, I crawled into my upper bunk. If you've never slept in a trucker's cab then don't ever take up the opportunity if it's offered to you. Don, wisely, claimed the lower bunk, situated behind the driver and co-driver seats. I had the upper bunk. It was reasonably soft, but you have to be a contortionist to get into a sleeping bag while at the same time step up and slide yourself into the space between the bunk and the roof of the cab. By the end of our stay I had it worked out. But they were the most uncomfortable nights of my life because the cabin roof was only two feet away from my face and turning over became a tricky operation because my shoulder would graze the roof each time - and there was always the possibility of slipping over the edge!

I also got used to sleeping in perpetual daylight. There was no putting the lights out at night because outside we had the stadium floodlights blazing directly into our camp - for security purposes. Also, all through the night, a distant sound vibrated in the air, a moaning sound that sometimes sounded like singing. I later discovered the sound came from a group of women who maintained a 24-hour prayer vigil in one of the rooms under the main stand and they were the unseen pillars to the glorious crusade that was to begin the following afternoon.

The next day Reinhard and the ministry team arrived at Lubumbashi airport and I was among those who went to meet him. With us was Ronald Monot, who had arranged for Reinhard to meet the city commissioner. Six of us squeezed into a vehicle designed for four people and headed for the offices of the Commissioner, Mr Kasitaki.

We were cordially received at the commissioner's office and through an interpreter Reinhard conveyed his warm greetings and desire to share the gospel of hope and peace with the people of Lubumbashi. The Commissioner pointed out that Reinhard was following in some illustrious footsteps - Pope John Paul II had been a visitor to the city only a week earlier. In fact, one of the local newspapers, *Taifa*, had carried adverts concerning the Pope and the CFAN crusade on facing pages.

After the courtesy visit I joined Reinhard and the

rest of the ministry team at the Monot household. The Monots provided sleeping accommodation for Reinhard and the rest of the ministry team. I must confess I cast an envious eye at the sight of the beds my colleagues would be sleeping in!

The first day of a crusade is always a thrill and by two o'clock the first people began arriving and an hour later the huge covered stand on the west side of the ground was filled. The crowd soon overflowed onto the main playing field and an estimate put it at close to 70,000.

They were an excitable, noisy crowd and Reinhard had great difficulty in "reaching" the crowd that afternoon. Whether it was the new interpreter or just a spiritual blockade it was one of the shortest sermons I have ever heard Reinhard deliver. When he had finished he prayed a general prayer for the sick and then asked for those touched by the Lord to come forward. What followed was chaos.

The people didn't seem to understand properly what had been said and a stampede of people moved toward the platform. Among them were people who had been healed, but others wanted to get to the platform for a personal "blessing" from Reinhard, proabably a carryover from the recent visit by the Pope.

The situation became almost dangerous as the mob began to crush up against the platform, including women and young children. I had to abandon my job of taking photographs to help drag young children up onto the platform, who were being crushed against the poles. The platform became a place of refuge, with the sick, lame and healed trying to escape the surging, pressing crowd. Clouds of dust filled the air and after only a few testimonies, Reinhard decided to abandon the platform and let the crowd dismiss.

It had been impossible to control the altar call and to get the people to the counsellors and the meeting broke up in general disarray. Nevertheless, the gospel had been preached with power and might, and many miracles of salvation and healing had taken place.

That evening an emergency meeting was held between Reinhard, Peter Vandenberg and Kobus, and some of the local people, to see what could be done to control the crowd. This was the first time in CFAN's crusade history that crowd control had completely broken down and failed.

On the advice of the locals it was decided that the only choice was to have a row of gendarmes in front of the platform, assisted by our own ushers, who would try to keep some order and control, helping people with genuine testimonies to get to Reinhard on the podium. Nobody was keen about the idea of having uniformed policemen on duty, but it seemed that this was the only form of discipline that the people would respond to.

The gendarmes were very much in evidence throughout the city, and one could hardly travel a single street block without encountering a couple of the constabularly, who periodically halted cars, checking for licences, personal tax clearances and overloading, the latter being the most common offence and was usually taken care of by a few bank notes passed swiftly and silently. It was obvious, though that scant attention was given to road worthiness of the vehicles. If they had the transport system of the city would have ground to a permanent halt.

So for the rest of the crusade a platoon of gendarmes took up positions each day in front of the platform and crowd control became manageable, although a follow up to the altar call had to be abandoned because of the huge numbers that responded, and also because we were informed that street numbers for homes in many parts of the city did not exist! Hard to believe, but not uncommon in Africa, where some of the disciplines of the western lifestyle don't seem to be so important.

After another cramped and cold night - the days were blazingly hot, but temperatures dropped dramatically in the early hours of the morning - I was confronted by one of the washer women, who insisted I take a picture of a friend of hers who had been healed in the midst of the chaos of the previous day. With the washer woman as our guide a colleague and myself drove through the narrow, dusty alleys that criss-crossed the suburb we were in to find the home of the young woman.

It transpired that the woman, 23-year-old Ngoy Kasongo, had been carried by her mother and sister to the stadium on the previous afternoon. She had been bedridden for two years. When I visited her home she shyly came out of the dark, windowless, unplastered house to face the camera. She walked across the sandy yard, without stumbling, although she was still weak from many months in bed.

Her mother was still beaming and through a Swahili interpreter I got the young woman's simple story, that as she lay on the hard, grassy ground at the stadium she had suddenly felt strength flowing into her body. "It entered my whole body ... from my head to my feet and this power lifted me up and I went forward to the platform. I was bewildered at first ... then I gave God the glory," explained Miss Kasongo, as a crowd of neighbours gathered to hear the story and enter into the praise and thanksgiving that had filled that simple home. As I was to see later in the afternoon, many miracles had happened and many more were about to shake the Mobutu Sese Seko stadium.

Although the crowd was smaller, about 50,000, it was a meeting marked by some outstanding testimonies of the sovereign move of God's Spirit among the people. Reinhard was more relaxed as he preached, but it was a bold message and tough on sin. One hoped that some of the thousands of children among the crowd would hearken to the gospel! They continued to be unruly and because of the dryness of that time of the year - the rains were not due for another six weeks - the playing field of the stadium was losing a lot of its grass and there were several, large bare patches where the children deliberately picked up handfuls of sand and threw it in the air or at people.

One of the amusing pictures I have in my mind is of Roger West at his sound control panel about 100 yards in front of the platform and slap in the middle of the crowd. At the close of the meeting the crowd would invariably start dancing and praising the Lord, sending up a cloud of dust that even dimmed the floodlights. In the middle of this sat Roger, desperately trying to protect his equipment from the fine dust and sometimes disappearing from view as a fresh squall of red dust drifted over him.

No attempt was made on the second day at an altar call. Those wanting to receive Jesus were asked to raise their hands and say the sinners prayer where they stood and hopefully Christians standing nearby made contact with them to follow up and to get them into fellowship with other Christians. It was unsatisfactory, but we had to trust them to the Holy Spirit, to truly be their Comforter and Guide.

The testimonies of healing could have gone on all night, and the impact of the crusade was reaching into every corner of the city. Crusade Director Chris Lodewyk had some exciting news in the evening when he disclosed that Zaire television were keen to do a direct broadcast from the stadium. A direct radio broadcast was also planned. Besides this the television producer, a Christian, wanted to have Reinhard and others of the team, on a discussion programme on Friday night. The Lord was opening every conceivable door to get the gospel published in Zaire.

The outside broadcast vans of Zaire Television arrived early on Friday morning and they began rigging up their equipment and cables for the afternoon transmission, but due to some technical difficulties they were unable to get a picture transmitted and only the sound went out. Maybe it was providential because the crowd was the smallest of the crusade - about 35,000 people.

Among those at the meeting, and highly impressed and touched by the word of God, was the local "mayor". He was able to see and check for himself some of the many blind and deaf who experienced healing during the afternoon. I know it may sound blasé, but healings and miracles are almost common place in Africa, where the belief in the supernatural is so much stronger than those brought up in the so-called scientific western culture.

There was one incident during the service, when Reinhard demonstrated his control and authority over the powers of darkness. It happened just after he'd finished preaching and praying for the sick. He was urging those who knew they'd been touched by Jesus to come forward to the microphone, when a tall, sharp-featured woman, neatly dressed in a traditional long kaftan, came strutting and shoving her way through the crowd.

Her arms were up-raised and at first glance it appeared as though she was praising the Lord. The reaction of the crowd, of course, was to begin to applaud, but as she drew nearer, Reinhard, detected she was not praising God for her healing, but in fact, was under the control of an evil spirit. Boldly, he said it into the microphone and some of the CFAN team stopped her from getting to the platform. Immediately she became convulsed and started screaming. Ushers carried her away and prayed for her deliverance from evil spirits.

It was an incisive bit of spiritual discernment, because the woman could have thrown the whole meeting into confusion if she had been allowed to get to the microphone. This is one of the hazards of crusade work in Africa, where the preacher has to depend upon the Holy Spirit, and not his deacons or elders to filter out the troublemakers.

That evening Reinhard, Mike Kolisang, Peter, Chris, and Ronald Monot were on television. We managed to borrow an old TV set which was rigged in the kitchen and I and the team jammed in around the table to watch the show. The slot lasted 20 minutes and besides telling the audience about CFAN and the vision for Africa, Reinhard prayed for the sick, for the city and for the nation. The show was hardly off the air when the telephone calls started pouring into the studio to tell of sicknesses disappearing after Reinhard's prayer. One caller, from Kolwezi, about 200 miles north west of

Lubumbashi, pleaded for CFAN to come to his town and hold a crusade.

All the meetings were scheduled to begin at 3 o'clock each afternoon because the authorities were not keen on mass meetings running late into the night, but on Saturday, the starting time was switched to 5 o'clock because the city Commissioner had declared a "clean-up day". A curfew was placed on any traffic passing through the city between two o'clock and five o'clock in the afternoon. If you had to travel in the afternoon then you had to get a special police permit, otherwise you stood a good chance of having your vehicle impounded and spending the weekend in jail. The residents of the city were all expected to help in cleaning the city pavements and streets.

That Saturday morning Peter called a special staff meeting, held in the kitchen-cum-TV-room-cum-boardroom, during which proposals for the impending move to Harare were to be aired. Before the discussion there was a devotional time, which in hindsight, was of considerable significance.

Peter shared some thoughts based on the Scripture 2, Samuel 24:24, *"However, the King* (David) *said to Araunah, 'No but I will surely buy it from you for a price, for I will not offer burnt offerings to the Lord my God which cost me nothing.' So David bought the threshing floor and the oxen for 50 shekels of silver."* (Open Bible). Peter's theme for the morning devotion had been on sacrifice and the price that each one of us was prepared to pay to follow Jesus, possibly in view of the hardships and difficulties that CFAN would encounter as they reached deeper into Africa.

Peter, normally smiling and cheery, was unchar-acteristically tearful and choking in his voice when he posed the question: "Are we ... am I ... prepared to sacrifice my life ...?" It was a sombre moment - but only a brief one because, as so often happens, the mind dismisses thoughts of death. There is always that thought that it "won't happen to me". Yet in that crowded kitchen that morning two men, two of our brothers in Christ, two men we loved and worked with, were going to make the ultimate sacrifice in the cause of the gospel.

Reinhard arrived later at the meeting and announced that because of the need to assist in the follow up work, he and the ministry team would be staying on three extra days to preach in the churches and encourage the thousands of new converts to join up with a church.

It was another searing day and with the meeting starting much later I decided to try and catch up on some much-needed sleep. I climbed onto one of the bunks in the sleeping container and tried to doze, but it was impossible. A steel container, parked out in the open sun, is the closest to a sauna. As I lay on the bunk, the perspiration burst out on my forehead and then suddenly a clammering of feet on the ladder shattered my drowsiness. It was the tall, mustachioed Albert, who burst through the doorway and flung himself down on his bunk. He had just been given the news that his father had passed away at his home in Cape Town. I spent some time comforting and praying with Albert and then withdrew to leave him alone with his grief.

Stepping outside into the dazzling sun I was amazed to see that at least 200 people were already sitting on the grass near the front of the platform. I walked towards them and saw that most of them were elderly or sick. Some could not walk, others were blind or deaf. It was a pathetic sight - and it was only 1.30 pm.

This group sat there in the scorching heat all afternoon, not moving, or seeking to find any shade. They brought no food or water with them and we gave them bottles of fresh water during the afternoon. Looking at those people, I was again deeply touched - and hurt. These people were desperate for good health and were willing to sit all afternoon on the hard, dusty ground in blazing heat to listen to the gospel and, hopefully, reach out to Jesus to make them whole in spirit and body. I thought how impatient I often got when sitting in the comfortable, air conditioned waiting room of my local doctor!

Despite it being a Saturday night, with the obvious counter attractions of the local nightclubs, the stadium filled up with a crowd of about 50,000. Reinhard preached a short message so as to give more time for testimonies, because it was obvious that the number of healings was far exceeding anything we had seen in Lusaka. Faith was high and the testimonies were helping build up the people to see Jesus not only as Saviour, but as Healer.

There was one note of discord at the service and that was again caused by the children. Because the meeting started later than usual the children had flooded the field and started various little football matches among themselves. Most times they didn't even have a proper ball to kick around, but only one made from old rags tightly bound together with some string and twine.

When the meeting started repeated requests were made for the children to stop playing on the far side of the field, but to no avail. It was noticeable that neither the adults, nor the gendarmes, did anything to control the children, who continued playing, and also enjoying the privilege of having the floodlights on once the sun had gone down.

So all the while that Reinhard preached, about 400 children shouted, screamed and dashed around the far side of the field, kicking up dust and enjoying their game. On one occasion I walked around to the far side of the field, hoping to persuade the youngsters to show some respect, while the message was being preached, but they started off their good-natured chant of "meester, meester" and I finished up kicking a few rag balls as well!

While among the children, one smudge-faced boy of about eight years old, suddenly clasped my hand and began to deliberately touch the skin on my hand and forearm. Fortunately an adult was nearby, who understood some English and I asked him to enquire what the little boy wanted. I was taken aback by the reply: "Oh, he just wants to feel a white skin!"

Only then did it occur to me that white-skinned people were an oddity here and that I had mistakenly taken it for granted that the local people were accustomed to seeing whites around. But not so, especially for a child, living in a poor suburb. I discovered that of the 750,000 population in Lubumbashi, there were only 3,000 Whites. I was definitely a rare bird!

The next day, Sunday was the closing service and after breakfast Reinhard and the ministry team came to the site where we shared a communion service in the kitchens. There was also a change of plan. Reinhard and the ministry team would not be staying on for the extra days, but the Monday meetings at three separate venues had already been announced and members of the Tech team were asked to volunteer to take these meetings. The choice fell on chief electrician Milton Kasselman, Chris Alberts, and myself. Milton, although involved the following day with the break down of the camp, was eager to minister because he was considering studying further at a Bible school in America, with a view to fulltime ministry.

The closing meeting was a joyful occasion with dozens again charging up to get to the microphone to tell the crowd of about 60,000 what Jesus had done for them. One was an elderly woman, who came to the meeting almost doubled over and hobbling on a stick. She told the cheering crowd that she had been healed by Jesus and to prove it threw her stick away and walked upright along the platform. Her joy overcame her when Reinhard took her hand and the pair began dancing before the Lord.

In fact, it was a week of vivid memories of great testimonies of the power of God. A skinny little girl in Reinhard's arms, smiling happily, because her lame limbs had been healed. Of the blind and deaf, rushing onto the stage eager to prove they could see and hear. Of the child running among the crowd at the back of the stage, with her mother trying to catch her. The child was so excited to be able to run and jump like other children, after having been partially paralysed.

The most dramatic healing was of a boy of about 12 years old. His mother told the audience that her son suffered from a crippling hip condition which made it impossible for him to walk in an upright condition. He couldn't run, jump or play sport, but even as she told Reinhard these facts her son was standing upright, bouncing like a rubber ball. In fact, he couldn't keep still for a moment and did a series of leaps into the air to show what Jesus had done for him. The joy that we shared with this mother and son was exhilarating. Just this one experience made the long, hard journey seem more than worthwhile.

When the Saturday meeting closed Reinhard strode across to the stalwart band of prayer warriors, who had gathered at the back of the platform and spoke to them and then laid hands on them, blessing them for their unseen, but valiant and powerful contribution to one of CFAN's most Holy Spirit-charged crusades.

The Sunday meeting was televised "live" and the next day we heard exciting reports from people who had stayed at home to watch and who had been healed when Reinhard prayed for the sick. Many of the TV sets were on in the local hospitals throughout the Shaba province and for weeks afterwards reports drifted in of people touched by the Lord and made well as they lay in their hospital beds.

Monday started for me at 3.00 am. My driver, Don, who is also a qualified pilot, was going to fly back south with Peter Vandenberg (also a qualified pilot) and our video man Eugene Würslin. I had to drive Don out to the Monot's home to collect Peter and Eugene and take them to the airport.

It was still dark when we set off in an open van through the deserted streets of Lubumbashi. I was pleased to see that no gendarmes were around. Earlier in the week we had suffered the misfortune to be stopped by the police, who had demanded to see Don's driving licence - he was at the wheel. Explanations had been difficult and after much hand-waving it was obvious the gendarme was going to be sticky about seeing Don's licence, which unfortunately, was back at the CFAN camp.

We proffered somebody else's licence and offered

to swap drivers, but the policeman became louder and more officious. Fortunately Ronald Monot arrived on the scene, a small attaché case under his arm in which he usually carried a bulky supply of banknotes. A brief consultation and we were waved on. Monot's attaché case had saved the day!

Now, as we drove through the poorly lit street - most of the street lights were broken, or did not have light bulbs in them - I was thankful that the coast was clear of any uniformed men. Then I realised I would have to drive the van back through the city later on in the morning, probably at peak hour. The thought did not charm me.

After making a suitable enough noise we managed to rouse Peter and Eugene and after loading a 44 gallon drum of aviation fuel onto the back of the truck we left for the airport. The fuel tanks were topped up and all the luggage and video equipment stowed away. Just on six o'clock, with the fiery red sun creeping up over the African bush, the tiny Maul aircraft clawed itself into the air and headed south.

Unfortunately, I could not return directly to the CFAN camp, but had to make a trip to the Monot's residence to return the empty fuel drum and my chances of getting through the city ahead of the peak traffic were slim. Traffic in Zaire travels on the right-hand side of the road, as in America, and the truck I was driving was a right hand drive and this fact made me the most defensive driver in the city that morning. But I prayed and drove carefully, especially around the wide circles, which one was tempted to go around the wrong way!

Finally, returning to the camp, I found the men busily dismantling the camp. Before he'd left Don had asked me to take charge of breaking down and packing the water purification plant and I was hoping that I might dodge this task because my mechanical knowledge is rather dubious. But when I saw how hard the team were engaged in their tasks, I decided that I had better make an effort to take apart the jig-saw of pipes and connections. With some help from my colleagues I did complete the job, but was drenched in the process.

The preaching engagements of the three "volunteers" were scheduled for four o'clock that afternoon and it was agreed that I should prepare a sermon outline for Chris and Milton, in particular, who could not leave the tough physical work of disconnecting all the wiring. Just before four o' clock, Milton, amazingly transformed from the hot, grimy artisan I had seen earlier perched on top of one of the lighting masts, presented himself at the door of my truck bedroom, for his notes.

Dressed in grey longs, a crisp white shirt and a huge Bible under his arm, he looked the part of a preacher and I wondered whether this afternoon might not be the start of a new call on his life. Later that night Milton returned from his preaching venue, beaming and thrilled. He'd had a congregation of about a 1,000 people to minister and teach the Word of God to. His eyes were dancing with joy and I think he took a firm decision that evening to go to Bible school to study to become a fulltime preacher.

Chris also reported a grand hallelujah meeting of close to a 1,000. His meeting had been in Ronald Monot's tent, which was pitched next to his residence. Chris has subsequently left for Bible school in Dallas, Texas. I had taught in the "Jerusalem" church in the city to a full house of 500, and after sharing the Word for about an hour was beseiged by people needing counselling and prayer for sickness. The needs, not only to evangelise, but to care for the saints, are truly great and desperate in Africa.

By the time we got to camp, dinner had been served and finished, and I had to be content with several slices of bread, peanut butter, jam and a little ice cream somebody had saved. Fortunately, we received freshly baked white bread each day, courtesy of the nuns at a local convent. The ice cream, from a small shop in the city, was also delicious and a real luxury, where sweets and chocolates are practically unobtainable.

One afternoon while sitting in the truck cab, busily opening a toffee I'd brought with me from down south, a young boy raced across the grass to me. In his hand was a small frog, beautifully carved out of green malakite stone. He jabbered away in French and I gathered he was prepared to swop the ornament for my toffee. I gave him a toffee and told him to keep his frog.

After washing down my "dinner" I was exhausted and in desperate need of sleep again. And with Don gone, I not only had the cab to myself, but I could sleep on the more spacious lower bunk. What luxury! I was learning that values soon change when you're in the heart of Africa.

Chapter 9

Death on the road

THE camp siren sounded at 5.00 am. It was Tuesday, September 3rd, 1985. A beautiful clear day. The air was clean and crisp as I washed my face and beard - I'd decided it was impossible to shave in cold water and grew a salt and pepper beard - in a dish of water next to my truck. The long haul back home started today. Fortunately I would only travel as far as Lusaka, in Zambia, with the trucks. I was scheduled to catch a commercial flight which left Lusaka on Wednesday at 2.30 pm.

Everybody was hard at work, stowing the last few items and checking that the trailers were all coupled and ready to roll. After a snappy breakfast the team gathered on the stadium field, just behind the goalposts, and sang a chorus. We joined hands and prayed for a safe journey that day.

I dare say that there is often a certain perfunctoriness attached to prayers for a safe journey and although I know that each one of us knew the necessity of such a prayer, maybe we did not attach sufficient significance or faith to it. I know that as I stood in that circle that morning, the air still cool, I had an urge to add a prayer, based on Psalm 91, to those already offered. I felt that those prayers already uttered, had not been powerful enough. Then I thought I was being vain and before I could come to a decision about praying or not, the meeting broke up. As events unfolded later that day I wondered whether my prayer would have had any influence on the chain of circumstances that awaited us only 115 miles down the road on the Zambian side of the border. It's a searching question and the answer will only be given to me when I see Jesus.

After some embracing farewells with Ronald and Sheila Monot and dozens of other Christians who came to the ground, the convoy of trucks and caravans pulled out of the Mobutu stadium, which was to be the venue for an international football match that coming Sunday and groundsmen were busily watering and trying to repair the surface which had been badly damaged by the thousands of people who had attended the crusade. It was 7.30 am as we circuited our way through the city, causing minor traffic jams and getting lots of "hallelujahs" and shouts of acclamation from the people who lined the streets.

Occupying the driver's seat in my truck now, was Gerry Davies, a tall blond-haired fellow who had been a co-driver on one of the other vehicles on the journey from Lusaka to Lubumbashi. Despite the deterioration of the road on some sections where the tar had completely broken up and been swept away, and the usual roadblocks, we were at the Kasumbalesa border post at ten o'clock.

Chris Alberts patiently and meticulously went through all the papers with the customs officials and after a few routine arguments that become part and parcel of border crossings in Africa, the convoy jerked off down the road at 1.10 pm. We had been at the border post for over three hours.

As the caravans led by Chris Alberts in a Toyota

sedan pulled off, the five trucks were supposed to set off in a pre-arranged order, but because of the frustration of the delay at the border, the drivers pulled off just as soon as they got into their cabs and down the road.

While at the border Kobus had wanted the truck I was in to be the lead truck, because we were the slowest of the five. But this did not happen. Instead, Gerhard Ganske stayed as the lead truck, followed by Englishman Kim Fullam, then Horst Kossanke with Milton Kasselman as his co-driver, then myself and Gerry Davies with Friedhelm Wentland, in the last truck. Bringing up the tail was the young German, Jurgen Rudolph, driving a 10-seater bus.

I was still standing outside the customs building when the first of the trucks pulled away so I ran across towards mine, passing in front of Horst Kosannke's truck as he swung the wheel around. Milton smilingly waved at me as I passed his side of the truck. It was the last time I saw either of them alive.

After another brief stop at a police check the convoy got rolling. We planned to go straight through and make Lusaka by midnight. The road we were travelling on was fully tarred, but narrow. Yet sitting high up in the cab of this powerful vehicle, I felt absolutely secure as smaller cars and trucks passed us by. There was a feeling of power and immunity from other vehicles as the needle on the speedometer hovered close to the 80 kph. On each side of the road, tall grass waved back and forth from the wind caused by the slipstream of the trucks ahead of us. Stretching out before us were some huge slime dams from the nearby Konkola copper mine.

During the rainy season a lot of this slime runs off into the bush and during the prolonged, dry months this thin covering of slime breaks up to form a fine, white, powdery dust.

As Gerry and I chatted I noticed a heavy truck and trailer coming towards us at high speed. I knew it was travelling fast by the way the trailer was snaking behind the horse and I began to flinch as it neared us. It whizzed past safely and I took a big breath of relief. But not for long because another truck and trailer was pounding towards us.

Being a left-hand drive Gerry was keeping to the extreme edge of the narrow road, so as to give the oncoming vehicle all the extra room on the crown of the road. As this second truck hurtled down on us, I thought, for a fleeting moment that we were going to collide and I braced myself for an impact.

There was a terrific explosion right next to my ear. I looked up at Gerry, who glanced at me in bewilderment for a second and then we realised that the wing mirrors of the two trucks had touched. I adjusted the mirror, which was amazingly unbroken. Then I saw a third truck coming towards us.

I must confess that Psalm 91 was working overtime in my mind and my knees were distinctly weak, but as I looked again at the oncoming truck I relaxed. This driver, obviously having encountered the rest of our convoy and aware of how narrow the road was, had pulled over onto his extreme left and was travelling with one wheel off the tar, leaving, of course, a good safety margin in the centre of the road.

Unfortunately though, this driver's safety-first precaution caused an even greater hazard. The multiple wheels of his rig were billowing up dense clouds of fine, white dust and a light breeze was blowing it into the centre of the road.

Because of the hazard caused by the oncoming

trucks, my driver Gerry had slowed down and we no longer had the rest of the convoy in view. Now, with this huge dust cloud drifting down the centre of the road, visibility was greatly reduced.

The third truck passed by safely and then our vehicle plunged into the cloud of dust. Fear struck my heart immediately because we could not see more than a yard in front of us. I remember Gerry calling out: "Man, this is dangerous, I must slow down." And he began to ease the brakes on and gear down. We were in the middle of this dense dust cloud for only seconds and then we burst out into the bright sunlight. I blinked. I could not comprehend the sight that met my eyes. I was conscious, though, of Gerry braking hard and saying: "What's happened here?"

Directly in front of us, little more than 50 yards away, was a huge, red-painted cylindrical fuel tank, lying just off the centre of the road. To the right of it was a dark mass of metal, which I could not identify. On the left and a few yards past the red fuel tank was the trailer and the red-painted container behind Horst Kossanke's horse, which I could not see.

The trailer was half off the road and tilted at quite a steep angle. I was totally confused by what I saw, but as we jerked to a halt my mind flashed to that deadly dust cloud behind us and Friedhelm's truck thundering through it.

I yelled to Gerry to switch on his emergency lights and I began to climb down out of the cab, expecting at any second to hear and feel Friedhelm's truck ploughing into the back of our trailer.

Once my feet hit the tarmac I ran towards the silent scene of wreckage, still not comprehending what had happened.

In my mind I figured there'd been an accident and

that Horst had stopped his vehicle on the side of the road to give assistance. I deduced this from the way the trailer, with the containers on it, appeared to be neatly parked off the edge of the road and also because it seemed impossible for any vehicle to have got past the giant red fuel tank which blocked most of the road. As I ran towards the red fuel tank I noticed diesel spilling out onto the road. The tank was also punctured on top and a fine jet of diesel was spurting skywards. By now I could see smoke and flames further up the road and also small flames licking around the base of the tank.

I ran to the right hand side of the road to get a view of the road ahead, and was just in time to see the back of Kim Fullam's truck disappear over a rise. I then turned to look at the dark, metallic mass that had baffled me and realised that it was a trailer and part of a truck. I gazed again at the red fuel tank and then suddenly noticed, lying in a pool of diesel fuel, the crumpled body of a black woman with flames beginning to run towards her.

I'd jumped out of the truck without shoes and now realised I'd better get them back on before trying to run into any flames. As I ran back down the road I saw Friedhelm, who had stopped a safe distance behind our truck and the rest of our party who were in the mini-bus. I shouted to Friedhelm to get the woman away from the fuel tank and he and someone else picked her up and carried her a safe distance away, leaving her on the side of the road. All of this happened within less than two minutes.

By the time I had my shoes on the rest of our men had dragged out all available fire extinguishers and one was shoved into my arms. We galloped to the left-hand side of the road where the CFAN containers were being threatened by the spreading fire. Flames and great plumes of smoke were everywhere. A group of us battled through the tall, dry grass to get a side view of our trailer and then the full horror of what had happened hit me.

The CFAN truck and cab were completely demolished and totally engulfed in roaring flames that leapt high into the air. There was no sign of life. Somewhere in that inferno were Horst Kosannke and Milton Kasselman.

Kevin Royston, who had taken his holiday and joined the team from Harare to help with the sound system, tried to get closer to the fiery wreck with one of the fire extinguishers. It was an act of sheer desperation because the flames and the heat were so intense that the puny little extinguisher would have made no impression whatsoever.

Even as Kevin crawled forward there was an explosion, possibly one of the tyres. Kevin retreated and we stood in the tall, waving grass, completely helpless.

Three of our team, Ours, Albert and the cook Charlie, stood a little behind me under the shadow of a giant antheap and began to wail and cry for their brothers.

For a moment or two I stood paralysed. What does a Christian do in a disaster situation like this? For a moment I lifted my eyes to the blue skies above and plaintively prayed for a miraculous shower of rain to put out the flames. Five or six minutes had pasted and there was little prospect of anything surviving those devouring flames, which by now engulfed the whole wreck and a sinister black pall of smoke drifted silently up into the air.

I stared at the CFAN container with the words

"Jesus, Light of the World", smudged over by the black smoke. My prayer, I realised, was futile and I began to pray in tongues because my mind certainly did not have the answer.

Standing in the tall grass I was suddenly aware of another danger. The flames were now spreading from the wreck and into the brittle-dry grass. Diesoline was spilling down the road and into a gully which ran alongside the edge of the roadway. I immediately sensed a threat to our two trucks and minibus. They were in danger, and so were we, of being trapped by a wall of flames on each side of the road.

I rushed down from my vantage point and shouted to my colleagues to help me divert the river of diesoline into the bush so that we would be clear of the possible threat of flames on at least one side of the road. The drivers also backed away because the huge red fuel cylinder was now burning fiercely and for all we knew might explode.

During the panic and frantic efforts to do something to stop the fire, I had glimpsed out of the corner of my eye the starkness of the tragedy in human terms. Travelling in our section of the convoy was Horst's 19-year old son Rudi. When he arrived at the scene he immediately recognised that it was his father's truck. He rushed past me screaming, "Where is my father, where is my father?". I saw him a few moments later, wild-eyed and ripping his shirt in anguish.

That scene had only been a fragment of the drama that we were all involved in, but now as the truth began to sink in that our brothers in Christ were dead, it was now time to take stock and to care for the living.

I found Rudi sitting in the cab of Friedhelm's

truck. He was red-eyed and sobbing, but also full of rage and anger. I put an arm around him and prayed with him, speaking the comforting words of Jesus to him. No human words are ever adequate in such a situation.

Outside, the flames seared the sky and the black smoke which lifted high into the blue heavens was visible for many miles. Also, from nowhere, hundreds of people, mainly children, had appeared to chatter and watch the drama.

By now the rest of the convoy which had been ahead of us had stopped and some of the team had returned. Shock and dismay was on all our faces. Grown men cried unashamedly for their beloved brothers in Christ.

I remember walking along the side of the road with my arm around Werner Drotleff, who sobbed openly. Although deeply grieved myself, the Word of the Lord came strongly into my heart and it was simply this: "To be absent from the body is to be present with the Lord." I tried to comfort my colleagues and to lift their spirits with these words, but it was hard because all around us now was the smell of death.

That day was the longest and most trying of my life. The accident happened at about 1.30 pm and it was at least 90 minutes before a fire tender arrived from the nearby mine to douse the flames. Then came the gruesome task of removing the bodies and of trying to piece together how the accident had happened.

There was an unpleasant scene when a member of the local Red Cross arrived, smelling heavily of alcohol, began to drunkenly accuse us of smuggling ammunition. Among the team are several men, who have quick tempers and before they came to Christ, knew how to handle themselves physically. It was an amazing act of the grace of God that restrained them from flattening the Red Cross official!

There was also some over-officious action by the police, who threatened me because I was taking photographs of the accident scene, mainly for insurance claim purposes. Then there was the pressing crowd of spectators and one of our team members whose only concern was in getting to Lusaka! All in all nerves became ragged and edgy, from grief, frustration and aggravation.

It's in tight corners like this that one finds out just how much the Word of God controls your life.

In the middle of all this distress the Lord provided comfort, strength and practical help. Some of the spectators were more than just onlookers. Among them were a group of Christian women, who came to offer their condolences and to pray for us. Then some mine management officials arrived to offer any assistance that we might require and then a local farmer, Mr Erich Trytsman and his two sons, arrived to offer aid as well. They brought boxes of soft drinks which were greatly appreciated. Trapped on the middle of a boiling tar road for over five hours, with no shade, is in itself physically trying. The Trytsman family offered the CFAN convoy refuge on their nearby farm that night which was gladly accepted.

After seeing the wreckage cleared from the road, which was closed all afternoon and held up all traffic between Zambia and Zaire, we went to the farmhouse, which was on the banks of the Kafue River. We got there at seven o'clock that evening. We were all slightly numbed by the experiences of the day. Also in the convoy was Milton's younger brother Danie, who stood up to the tragedy with marvellous fortitude.

During the course of the afternoon Kobus notified Reinhard of the tragedy. Reinhard told him he would make plans to charter a flight to be with the team as soon as possible.

While the team sat around a long table in the large courtyard of the farmhouse, with the Trytsman family preparing a huge chicken barbecue, we sang songs of praise and began to pray for the wives and family of our departed brothers. The extent of the tragedy, as far as it affected loved ones, was only now beginning to impact upon us.

As we checked over the details of that afternoon we began to piece together what probably happened on that narrow bit of road at 1.30 pm. Kobus, who had been leading the convoy at the time, was the first to encounter the oncoming trucks and, noticing how fast they were travelling, had radioed back to some of the drivers who were also equipped with walkie-talkies. One of the men he spoke to was Milton, warning him to beware of the fast-approaching north-bound convoy. A minute after that conversation Milton and driver Horst were killed. Kobus had called again on his radio, but got no response from Milton. He thought maybe a small hill was hindering the radio signals. Only when he had seen the first whiffs of smoke did he realise something serious was wrong.

Nobody on earth will ever quite know what happened in those fateful moments. An inquest, at which I later appeared, put down the cause of the accident as "unknown" and held no person responsible for it. However, I am convinced that the pall of white, powdery dust was the key cause.

My deduction, based on what I saw immediately

after the accident and on subsequent investigations by insurance agents, is that when Horst entered the cloud of dust he kept his rig on the extreme left-hand side, which would be natural because it was a left-hand drive truck.

However, there was a slight embankment falling away on the left of the road and I believe that the trailer began to slide away, causing a slight jack-knifing, which Horst probably tried to correct by steering towards the right again. Simultaneously, the oncoming truck entered the same dust cloud. Knowing from our own experience just how limited the visibility was and how quickly one gets disorientated, I deduce that the driver of the north-bound truck wandered momentarily across the centre of the road and collided head-on with Horst, who was battling to control a possible jack-knifing.

The speed and the weight of the impact was horrendous in its devastation. The giant fuel tank broke loose and catapulted ahead of the moving truck, ripping off the cab in the process. The CFAN cab was crushed and buckled and the long-range fuel tanks ruptured. An electrical fire started immediately, which soon became an inferno.

From what remained of the charred bodies it was obvious that Horst died instantly behind the wheel, probably never knowing what hit him. But there is an unsolved mystery surrounding Milton's death.

His charred body was found lying stretched out next to the crumpled cab, the only physical injury a broken wrist. A passerby who arrived seconds after the impact, says he saw the "driver" of the CFAN truck run towards the cab and try to help "the other man". Then there was an explosion and he saw the "driver" fall onto the ground.

Of course, what the eye witness did not realise was that the truck was left-hand drive and he actually saw Milton trying to help Horst, who was behind the wheel. Milton's widow, Jane, has a theory that her late husband did try to help Horst, but collapsed and fainted when he saw the extent of his colleague's injuries. According to Jane, Milton could not stand the sight of blood and even a small cut suffered by his children would cause him to faint. So it would appear that Milton amazingly survived the impact, only to either be knocked out by the explosion or simply fainted and was burnt to death.

We ate at about 10.45 pm that evening - our first bite of food since leaving Lubumbashi early in the morning and then I joined the queue to have a hot shower the first in eight days! But it wasn't just the thought of the hot water. Having been around the fiery, and later, smouldering wrecks all day, the smell of diesel and death still clung to one's hair. A hot shower not only freshened me, but also washed away that lingering smell and I crawled into my cab bunk at about 11.30 pm.

Despite the ordeal I found I was wide awake and my mind racing over the events of the day. It was then, alone in that cab, that the horror of it all struck me. During the day I had been involved in comforting and generally trying to maintain a traditional stiff upper lip, but now, alone in my bunk, 4,000 kms away from my wife and two daughters, a chill gripped me. Yes, it could have been this very cab I was sleeping in that could now be lying, twisted and mangled, on the side of the road.

Also what hit me - and it impacted on a lot of the other married men - was the fact that Horst and Milton were now with the Lord, but their wives and children were left behind. They were the ones who really suffered the loss. They were the ones who made the real sacrifice. And I wondered whether any of the married men had ever looked at it in that light.

It was relatively "easy" to die for Jesus and give your life in the cause of His gospel, but had I ever really asked my wife and children if they were prepared for me to make that sacrifice? There is a sense of adventure for the men on this great gospel crusade in Africa. If sudden death came, as it had that afternoon, then it was all over and one was transported into the presence of Jesus. But a legacy of tears and anguish were left behind for the loved ones.

In my mental anguish I turned to my Bible and read a verse from Psalms that quietened my spirit: "Be not afraid of sudden disaster." An apt word for me that night. Lying in the pitch darkness, tears wetting my pillow, I thanked the Lord that I was alive to serve Him and to have the joy of seeing my wife and daughters again. In those moments life and my family were very precious to me. I also saw once again the futility of life without Christ. Horst and Milton hadn't died while delivering food or fuel or machinery. No, they had died in the line of duty for the God of this universe. It was a death worthwhile. No other cause, no matter how noble it may sound, can compare with that of the gospel. There is no greater honour than to live and to die for Jesus Christ.

I dozed off to have a peaceful six hours sleep. Plans for the new day were for Chris Alberts to take myself and Horst's son Rudi straight through to Lusaka. I was booked on the 2.30 pm flight for Johannesburg and arrangements were made to book Rudi on the same flight so that he could get home to his mother, Lydia, and younger brother Ingmar. Although both widows had already been told of the news, I would have to be the one to give them the details later that night.

After a farm style breakfast, the three of us left for the 290 mile journey to Lusaka. We pulled out of the Trytsman's farm at 8 o'clock, hoping to reach the Zambian capital just after noon, which would give me plenty of time to check in and make sure that Rudi's booking was in order.

However, our journey took over an hour longer because of several police road blocks and getting caught behind slow-moving traffic on some narrow stretches of road.

Rudi slept most of the time. He was in a semi-shocked state and was afraid to go home. The trauma of having to face his mother and younger brother, was obviously something which he felt he could not handle. However, I was able to encourage and build up some confidence in him, emphasising that his mother needed him at her side, especially as she was four months pregnant and needed every bit of moral fibre and strength to get her through the shock and trauma she was enduring.

As we sped along the road, I couldn't help but notice how I involuntarily stiffened each time I saw a big truck hammering towards us. Chris, at the wheel of the Toyota Corolla, also eased his foot off the pedal each time. We both recognised the impression left on us by the previous day, but decided that we would not allow ourselves to cower to any devilish deceptions of fear. I must confess that each time I see a truck coming my way, I have an instant recall of September 3rd, 1985. I'm not fearful when driving, but maybe it's lodged in my memory to remind me of how frail we are; like the grass of the field, blooming one day and withered and blown away the next.

The drive to Lusaka became a chase against the clock and we swung into the airport grounds at just after one o'clock, which gave us an hour to check in. All was well, I thought. I had my ticket, but I had to collect Rudi's at the passenger services counter. It was closed and did not open until 1.45 pm. It was going to be a close thing, but still, all I had to do was to collect the ticket. As soon as the counter opened I enquired for Rudi's ticket. There was no trace of it. A phone call to the city office. Had they received a telex about the ticket?

The booking was confirmed. Then a fumbling in a drawer to find a ticket. How do you spell the name? Interruptions from a businessman also trying to get onto a flight. Eventually I got Rudi's ticket and raced for the check-in counter. Sorry, closed. You've missed it! I looked at my watch. It was 2.20 pm. The plane wasn't scheduled to take off for another ten minutes. Anxious pleading and trying to explain the accident and reason why we must get on the flight. All right! We grabbed our boarding passes, filled in some immigration forms, paid our airport dues and raced for the stairs only to be halted by a customs official.

I had to open my suitcase and he went through it. Then Rudi had to open his. Lying on top of his clothing was a CFAN T-shirt with the wording "I love Jesus". The customs official smiled broadly. He was a believer too, and now hustled us off to sprint across the apron of the airport and clamber up the steps and into a seat. We'd made it, although the flight was 20 minutes late in taking off!

Ninety minutes later we touched down at Jan Smuts international airport. There, to meet us at the airport, was Reinhard's wife Anni, Rudi's brother

Ingmar, our financial director Claude Ansley and my wife Maureen and my daughters Tammy and Kerrie-Lee. It was a joyful reunion, but heavy with pathos in another way. We drove directly to the Witfield complex and I went first to Jane, Milton's widow. Members of her family had already arrived to be with her and I found her surprisingly strong and resilient and eager to hear me give an account of the events of the previous day.

From there I walked across to the home of Lydia, Horst's widow, and found her tearful, but also standing up under the sorrow, which seemed to be reinforced by her pregnancy and the fact that Horst would not see his unborn child. We prayed and talked for a while.

There was great concern for the unborn child, because earlier in the year Lydia had suffered a miscarriage and the present pregnancy had also suffered some early complications. But the Lord overshadowed her and in January 1986 she gave birth to a girl, Rebecca, in Stuttgart, West Germany, where she returned in December 1985.

Meanwhile, earlier in the morning, Reinhard and Peter, with pilot Ken Geldenhuys, flew up to the Zambian Copperbelt to be with the team. When he first received the news Reinhard had an immediate desire to be with his men. He met up with the convoy just outside of the town of Kitwe and they hugged and shed a few tears on the side of the road, where they prayed and comforted each other. With commendable assistance from officialdom, arrangements were made for the bodies to be flown out the next day.

On the return flight, Peter and Ken were up front and Reinhard shared the back seats with the remains of his two brothers in Christ. Speaking at the funeral, held in a tent on the Witfield office grounds a few days later, Reinhard recalled his thoughts as he sat in the back of the plane:

"It was like carrying the bones of Joseph back to the Promised Land, not that there was anything special in the bones, but there was a promise with them ... God would fulfil His Word. Yes, even over my own death and grave God will fulfil His Word for Africa to be saved!"

At the funeral Reinhard recalled a warning given by the Holy Spirit some two years earlier. "The Holy Spirit spoke repeatedly that a time would come when some of us would lay down their lives for the sake of the gospel. The Holy Spirit spoke of martyrdom ... the path we are treading is red with the blood of martyrs who have gone before us. But no matter what the price or cost this vision will find fulfillment - even if we back out, God will find someone else. But we will go this way until the end - until Jesus comes. The blood of the martyrs is the seed of the Church. The more Satan kills the saints the more God's people prosper, the more the Kingdom of God grows."

He made a direct challenge to all the CFAN team at the funeral: "We are not backing out from this divine call. If anyone says he cannot pay the price or the road is too rough, I will ask him to rather look for a more comfortable ministry. The road ahead is tough and rough, but at the same time glorious. I for one want to walk it to the end."

With such a challenge and the two coffins of their brothers in Christ before them with the South African and West German flags draped at the back of the podium, there was no one who could not say "amen" to the call to persevere.

The Zambia and Zaire crusades had been glorious

events, but at a price. Being involved in frontline crusade evangelism is not all "hallelujahs". The tears of joy can also become tears of sorrow.

Chapter 10

Race Course Crusade

The next major crusade in Africa was scheduled for the end of October in Accra, the capital city of Ghana. Ever since the Nigerian crusade Reinhard was keen to return to the populous west coast of Africa, where he sensed that God's harvest was ready to be reaped.

So, on October 29th, Reinhard and a small team arrived in the bustling city of Accra. Planning for the crusade had been initiated by CFAN organiser Ekkehard Hornburg, who had been assisted by local missionaries Frans and Esther Kleefeld, who were later to be appointed as CFAN's West African representatives. Altogether 25 churches and ministries joined hands to form the "Ghana Pentecostal Council", which invited CFAN to stage the crusade.

Two days before his departure for Accra Reinhard received a message informing him that permission to use the stadium in the centre of the city had been withdrawn.

This is a typical occurrence in Africa where decisions are changed overnight by officialdom, without taking cognisance of the planning and preparation which may have gone into an event. As it was, thousands of posters and handbills had been handed out for the crusade, and the Christians were eager that the crusade go ahead.

Despite the last minute confusion caused by the switch in venues, Reinhard agreed to hold the crusade. The alternative venue was an interesting one - the local race course!

Later on, when preparing an international Press Release on the Accra Crusade, I couldn't resist the following introduction: "In Revelation 19 we have the picture of the triumphant Lord Jesus Christ riding the white horse and in Accra the Saviour was again the winner when CFAN held a giant crusade on the local race course!"

The change in venue resulted in a slow start to the crusade, with only 20,000 people attending the first evening meeting. But the power of God was evident and as the good news spread through the city, the crowds grew bigger. Attendance doubled each evening and on the final night there was a crowd estimated at 120,000.

On the first evening five women testified of being healed of breast cancer and on the second night a mother rejoiced to see her four-year-old son, born blind, touched by the power of God. A 12-year-old girl, whose mother carried her on her back to the meeting, brought roars of applause when she began to jump up and down on the platform. Her mother told the audience that her daughter had been unable to walk for seven years.

There was one more meeting, held on the Saturday morning, under the blazing African sun. The meeting started at 8.00 am because there was to be a horse race meeting in the afternoon. Despite the early hour and the heat, crowds of people came to hear the gospel and turn to Jesus.

Reinhard's estimation of those who prayed the prayer of repentance and acceptance of Jesus during the five days was 70,000. His assessment of the ripe harvest had been spot on and he pledged then and there to have further crusades in Ghana. These followed early in 1986 in Kumasi, the second largest city in Ghana, situated about 120 miles inland from Accra and in March Reinhard preached in the smaller coastal towns of Takoradi and Sekondi.

The account of the Kumasi crusade, taken from CFAN's *Revival Report* magazine, makes exciting reading:

"The roar of the crowd was almost deafening. Without shame 100,000 voices were raised to proclaim the mighty power of God. As one pastor commented: "It felt as if the earth was shaking." And this sea of people had every reason to shout the praises of God when Jesus healed a blind woman during one of the evening services.

"The woman came up onto the platform and jubilantly told the crowd that she could now see. To test her out evangelist Reinhard Bonnke got her to follow his movements on the platform and then to describe his clothing. As she did this tears of joy and gratefulness to Jesus streamed down her cheeks - and the voice of the crowd rose in an anthem of praise.

"The Kumasi crusade in Ghana once again demonstrated the power of Almighty God to heal and set people free from their sins and bondage to habits and fetishes. On one night a dozen blind people received their sight and every testimony pulled at the heartstrings of the vast crowd. Truly, Jesus changed the night into day for these people.

"When Bro. Bonnke opened the service he told the people that the Lord had given him a promise that Jesus would open blind eyes during the course of the meeting. Before he began to preach all the blind people were called forward to the front where they sat on the ground near the big platform.

"After his message and an altar call which saw thousands come forward to receive Jesus as saviour, Bro. Bonnke instructed the blind people to place their hands on their eyes. He then told them he would command the blindness to go in Jesus' name and then they would open their eyes and see him on the platform.

"The chattering of the crowd almost ceased and for a brief, few moments silence, broken only by the booming voice of Bro. Bonnke, praying. Then there was holy pandemonium. Like lightning the healing power of God struck. Like great ocean waves the shouts of joy rolled over the stadium.

"Then Bro. Bonnke turned to the deaf and dumb. He asked co-evangelist Michael Kolisang to pray for these poor people and the result was amazing. Some, who had been born deaf and dumb, experienced complete healing and deliverance, through the power of Jesus' name.

"A mother cried with joy. Her eight-year-old daughter, a deaf mute, began speaking for the first time in her life, repeating the words, "Jesus is good". The pronunciation was so perfect that it was almost unbelievable - but true! Praise the Lord!

"It was as if the CFAN team had been transported back into the time of the apostles. The giant floodlights of the stadium, situated on a hill overlooking the city, seemed to symbolize that Jesus, the Light of the World, had come to Kumasi.

"The response to the preaching of the gospel was overwhelming. Nightly, crowds of up to 20,000 people called upon the name of the Lord to receive forgiveness from sin. It became impossible to have a conventional altar call as the crowd pressing forward was so great that there was just no space left in front of the platform. Only in heaven, where the book-keeping is correct, will we one day know the full number of those saved in Kumasi.

"Watching that human stream being born again to a living hope made the CFAN team realise again that this is the biggest and the everlasting miracle of the crusades. To win the lost for Jesus and to populate heaven.

"Day after day the crusade was big news in Kumasi. Hardly a single person among the 800,000 inhabitants was not aware that Jesus was visiting their city. Among those who took a keen interest was the king of the Ashantis, who was visited by Bro. Bonnke and the CFAN team.

"The giant stadium, which seats 80,000 people, had never before been used for a Christian event. It was not just used, it was filled to overflowing with 120,000 per service pressing in to hear the Good News.

"Pastor Opuni, of the Assemblies of God in Kumasi, who was chairman of the local crusade committee, commented:

'The whole city is vibrating with the news about the crusade. The meetings with Bro. Bonnke and his team are not only the greatest evangelistic gatherings that Kumasi has ever seen, but possibly the biggest for the whole country. A completely new and positive situation has arisen here. The spiritual climate has changed. We thank Jesus for this breakthrough.'"

The third major crusade in Ghana was held on a large open sportsfield midway between the towns of Sekondi and Takoradi.

Permission was granted for these meetings to be

held in the evening and advertised to begin at 7.30 pm, but by six o'clock streams of people filed into the grounds. During the five days the crowds varied between 60,000 and 80,000.

Ministers were amazed by the turnout because this was the first time that a large scale crusade had ever been held in the western region of Ghana.

According to one local pastor, Rev. Eogre Appekey, general secretary of the Assemblies of God and chairman of the crusade committee, the previous biggest gathering of Christians had attracted under 5,000 people.

There were so many sick people in the audience that it was impossible to lay hands on them individually, so one evening Reinhard called all the counsellors together and told them they were going to pray for the sick that night.

When the time came Reinhard told them to move into the crowd and lay hands on those who were sick and as they did so an anointing of the Holy Spirit fell on the crowd.

Seven blind people received their sight. Cripples tossed away their crutches and walked. A 20-year-old man, carried into the meeting, suddenly felt the power of God fall on him. He jumped up and ran to the platform to tell Reinhard what had happened. The young man had no shoes because he'd never had to wear them, so Reinhard gave him cash to go and buy a new pair for his newly healed feet!

Commenting on the crusade, Reinhard wrote in the German edition of *Missions-Reportage:*

"The peak of the crusade was without doubt the moment when Jesus baptised thousands of new converts with the Holy Ghost and Fire. It was like Pentecost in the Book of Acts. The Glory of the Lord came down like liquid fire. Many thousands received the gift of praising the Lord in a new language.

"The Western region of Ghana will never be the same because these people, ignited by the Holy Spirit, will carry the Fire everywhere. We are not ashamed of these wonderful manifestations of the Lord, no, we are grateful for them.

"We are seeing and experiencing what our prayer partners have prayed for so many years - revival!

"In Jesus' name it will continue through country after country. We can rest one day in Heaven, but now is the harvest time."

Chapter 11

Call From the East

A MAJOR departure from Reinhard's crusade calendar in Africa came in December 1985 when CFAN were invited to do a fullscale crusade in Singapore.

Reinhard had previously passed through Singapore on brief preaching engagements and had made such an impression on the local Christians that they begged him to return and stage a proper crusade. Although Reinhard has travelled the world and spoken on every continent, his big, city crusades have been held only in Africa.

Although flattered by the invitation, Reinhard was at first reluctant to get involved with a major crusade outside of Africa, but later agreed. The dates were set for December 11th to 15th inclusive and the magnificent, modern stadium was booked for the occasion.

Once Reinhard had given the green light, the Church in Singapore slipped into top gear and with typical oriental precision and diligence planned every fine detail. Assisting them with the know-how was Chris Lodewyk.

Since this was to be a full blown CFAN crusade it was decided that Suzette Hattingh should also go ahead and prepare the way with her intercessory prayer groups. This proved a great blessing to the saints there, who were challenged by the vitality of intercessory prayer.

A total of 70 churches co-operated, with the large and influential charismatic Anglican church, headed by Bishop Dr Moses Tai, playing a major role in the organising and preparation. Full page newspaper adverts were booked. Posters were placed in most public places and on buses. Special T-shirts were manufactured for the crusade.

Singapore, is a miracle nation because, despite its lack of size and absence of any natural resources, except its harbour and its strategic position in east Asia, is an exceptionally prosperous nation. It's a small, but crowded nation of 2.5-million people, consisting mainly of idol-worshippers (53.9%), Muslims (17.4%) and Christians (8.6%).

Despite being in the minority, the Christians of Singapore hold many high positions in business and commerce as well as in government circles. In fact, the Christians of Singapore are among the most affluent in the world! They have, thankfully, recognised that this temporal blessing is for the promotion of the gospel. Singapore is not only a nation and city of many religions, but also of cultures and languages, making its success as a unitary state even more remarkable.

It was also a test for Reinhard when he preached in the huge 70,000-seater stadium. He explains: "From the very first night I realised that there were many heathen in the stadium - people who had absolutely no Biblical knowledge. I was gripped by a deep urge to teach these dear people to know Jesus and His redemptive work on the Cross. And God's grace was with us. The Holy Spirit revealed Jesus and thousands of precious souls acknowledged Him as the Son of the Living God."

On the evening that Reinhard preached on the baptism of the Holy Spirit thousands experienced the reality of this wonderful Bible promise.

"Never before had we heard a whole stadium full of people singing in tongues", was the amazed comment of one Chinese organiser.

During this service there was a strange occurrence. As Reinhard preached on the Holy Spirit a large white bird suddenly flew into the middle of the stadium and hovered all the while within the arcs of the powerful floodlights. "It is a sign from God! The Holy Spirit is here," the people whispered to each other on the stands.

Later, when praying for the sick, Reinhard and Michael Kolisang saw cripples jumping out of wheelchairs and cancers disappear. "This is a breakthrough for Singapore," was the comment heard over and over again. "Never before has a crusade made such an impact," said Bishop Tai.

Besides the nightly crusades, Reinhard was invited to speak to 600 lecturers at the national university. This is the sort of invitation Reinhard delights in accepting. He's never intimidated by learned professors and delights to confound them with simple Bible truths.

The hall was overflowing with professors and lecturers, representing many religions. Reinhard, never ashamed to present the truth and claims of Jesus boldly and clearly, preached from Mark 15 on the heathen centurion who stood at the foot of the Cross and had the revelation that Jesus is the Son of the Living God. After Reinhard had challenged the lecturers the Holy Spirit moved wonderfully upon these learned men and a number responded to the altar call.

During the five-day crusade crowds of up to 50,000 came to the stadium and at least 7,000 registered firm decisions for Jesus.

The impact among the heathen was great and the Church in Singapore immediately asked Reinhard and his team to return again for a bigger crusade in 1987. Invitations to hold crusades in Malaysia and the Philippine Islands were also received, lifting the vision not only from Africa, but to Asia as well.

Chapter 12

Easter in London

VISITS to Britain have become a regular part of Reinhard's schedule and over the years he has been aware of a growing spiritual awakening in the nation that produced such great men as John and Charles Wesley, George Whitefield, George Müller, C.T. Studd, General Booth and many others, who made their mark in the Kingdom of God. Sadly, of course, Britain, like much of Europe, has slipped into the bondage of religious tradition over the past decades, losing the power of the gospel.

Over the past years though, Reinhard has been a regular campaigner in the British Isles, stirring up the Christians, giving them new-found faith to be bold and to dare to act on the Word of God.

Thousands of Britons have been set alight with a new vision, not only to support CFAN's great mission in Africa, but to challenge the people of their own nation with the power of the gospel.

Sometimes, though, even the men of faith and boldness, take a nosedive. Such was the case during Reinhard's visit in August 1984. While in Manchester the meeting became a bit chaotic. The hall was packed with people and it was desperately close and uncomfortable in the hall, so much so that an elderly man, with a bad heart condition, collapsed and died!

Then, while Reinhard was preaching a sermon

entitled "Turns" he twisted awkwardly while demonstrating his message and put his back out of place. He hung onto the pulpit and finished his sermon, but was in such pain that Peter Vandenberg had to help him off the stage and to the vestry. Reinhard couldn't even carry his briefcase. He had to fly to Germany the next day and he hobbled aboard the plane, looking like an old crippled man. On arrival in Frankfurt he went to a doctor for some injections and thankfully recovered. "I really had a picture of myself arriving at Jan Smuts airport in a wheelchair."

That was one UK trip that Reinhard preferred not to remember. But he was back again in 1985 to take the Easter Day service at the Royal Albert Hall.

This famous London venue was almost filled to capacity. According to locals it was one of the biggest religious gatherings since pre-war days. One elderly woman, who has been attending the Easter services at the Royal Albert for the past 50 years exclaimed: "It's the greatest meeting I've ever been to ... I'll never be the same again." The denominational news magazine *Elim Evangel* described the meeting thus:

"Crowds filled the platform, standing around the preacher. Crowds filled the area in front of the platform. Still more crowds filled the aisles stretching back through the building.

"People were going down like ninepins as they experienced God. Some wanted help to overcome a drug problem; others a sex problem; while others looked to God for a divine healing and many - there must have been hundreds of young people - simply stood as an act of commitment to Jesus."

As usual Reinhard's anointed preaching generated a high level of faith and an urgency to get involved with promoting the gospel. This was confirmed by a spokesman for the Elim Bible College who said that the number of applicants to join the college, following Reinhard's challenging message, "Faith Frightens Satan", rocketed. It was an Easter Service that few would ever forget. Reinhard's message that Jesus Christ is alive was etched deeply on the hearts and minds of the 6,000 faithful who were at the Royal Albert Hall.

In November 1985 Reinhard returned to England lighting further flames of revival. From the first meeting - held in the Watford Town Hall - it was clear that accommodating the crowds, was going to be a major problem. At the first meeting 250 people volunteered to leave, so as to allow visitors the opportunity to hear the preaching.

The next two meetings were held in Westminster Chapel, London, and this grand old building was filled to capacity. With uninhibited rejoicing the crowd witnessed how a young man, who had walked only on crutches for 30 years, began to take his first faltering steps, holding onto the pews. Reinhard's command to, "Let go the pews in Jesus' name!" resulted in him walking, then running down the aisles and finally leaping onto the platform holding his crutches aloft.

The King's Centre, in Aldershot, was the next venue and the jubilant and capacity crowd was requested not to "dance" on the balconies because of the danger of structural damage. Serious damage was done though - to the devil's domain, as men and women responded to the message of salvation.

A tightly packed schedule included meetings at the Central Hall, Birmingham, the Town Hall in Leeds, the large new Halton Pentecostal Church in Widnes, which seats 1,500 people, and the recently completed Leisure Centre in Newport, South Wales.

Such was the response to the ministry that at some meetings up to 500 people had to be turned away because of the rules governing crowd capacities. In the Leeds Town Hall a man received a mighty touch from the Lord and began pushing his own wheelchair up and down the aisles. He stood worshipping the Lord for the remainder of the service.

Truly, the winds of the Holy Spirit are sweeping through Britain and reports similar to this have been received from other evangelists who have recently been to the United Kingdom.

Chapter 13

Winning Australian Hearts

A COUNTRY which has taken Reinhard to their hearts is Australia. The Christian media have given his African exploits wide coverage and it was no surprise when he was asked to be one of the guest speakers at the 32nd World Convention of the Full Gospel Businessmen's Fellowship International, held in Melbourne, in March 1985. This convention followed hard on the heels of the mighty Ibadan crusade and Reinhard was fired up with a new drive and enthusiasm. The stories of the Nigeria crusade held the crowds spellbound.

His dynamic preaching also caught the eye of the secular press and the Townsville Bulletin devoted almost a whole page to an article on Reinhard, including five action photographs of him preaching as well as one of the dramatic crowd scenes from Ibadan.

The writer of the article, John Gagliardi, made these comments:

"Each night rallies were held in the huge Melbourne Sports and Entertainment Centre. It reputedly holds about 8,000 and was full every night. On the last night of the convention, it was standing room only. Officials estimated the crowd at more than 10,000. The big drawcard for the night rallies was a quietly spoken (at least when you met him face-to-face) German evangelist by the name of Reinhard Bonnke.

"Pastor Reinhard Bonnke is one of the world's leading evangelists and in terms of sheer numbers converted, probably the world's most successful in the past ten years. His home ground is Africa, where he is literally turning that continent upside down. And watching and listening to him in Melbourne, it is not difficult to understand that sort of result. His delivery is electrifying. His voice whispers one moment, then rolls like thunder, rocking the cavernous hall the next. During the Melbourne rallies at least 500 people went forward to be saved each night, with more than a thousand on the final night."

Interestingly there was another writer at the conference who was also observing the style and impact that Reinhard was making on the conference. He was Owen Salter, editor of an independent national Christian Magazine *On Being*, which treads warily when it comes to the charismatic Pentecostal movement, yet having a keen appreciation of their place in the Kingdom of God.

Mr Salter's observations and comments, made several months after the Melbourne meetings, are interesting coming from a man with an "orthodox" Christian background. Under the headline "Rompin' and Stompin' for Jesus", Mr Salter wrote:

"Reinhard Bonnke's preaching style wouldn't suit the normal parish pulpit. It wouldn't be big enough. Bonnke likes to stride around the stage, bend down low, throw his arms into the air like a triumphant boxer. He's celebrating victory - the victory of Jesus.

"Even when he's hoarse with laryngitis and speaking through a cranked-up PA, his thickly accented German-English accent has a penetrating quality. He's the only man I've heard who could shout in a whisper. And shout he does. It's one of his more common voice modulations. But Bonnke leaves even the most enthusiastic American evangelist for dead. The best I've ever heard from the Land of the Eagle was a big black preacher named E. V. Hill, whose delivery never dropped below 100 decibels, Bonnke used a wider vocal range and moved like an Indian rubber man with it.

"I encountered Bonnke in action on the stage at the Melbourne Entertainment Centre ... it was a remarkable experience. He preached for over half an hour, then invited people to come forward to receive Jesus or to be prayed for regarding healing or deliverance from spiritual affliction.

"It was a receptive audience - charismatic brothers and sisters from around the world, along with a large number of local Christians. Go forward they did. No doubt there were even some non-Christians in their number. But what happened next was totally unexpected. As he instructed those still in their seats to pray, he told the people who had come forward that a commitment to Jesus was all or nothing. It meant a complete break with their old life.

"So far so good. But then he said, 'I'm going to get you to throw onto the stage your cigarettes, your alcohol, your occult objects and I'm going to stomp on them in the name of Jesus!' Stomp on them? In the name of Jesus? Wait, I thought. Wait and see.

"An appeal for alcohol and occult objects at a world convention of the FGBMFI seemed to me a little, well, hopeful. Perhaps he'd failed to make the mental transition from non-Christian African crowds to an Australian Christian audience, I reasoned. I was prepared to allow him the possibility of a few cigarettes.

"Then an even more unexpected thing happened. He pointed to a part of the crowd to his left and said, 'God is telling me someone down here has an occult object. He wants you to throw it up onto the stage now!' Nothing happened. Then, after a few seconds, someone threw up a packet of cigarettes - from the outside of the crowd. Unfazed, Bonnke strode across. Exhorting his audience to unite their praise for victory while he proceeded to stomp on those cigarettes in the name of Jesus.

"Not just polite little steppings-on. Not even a vigorous grinding under the heel, but a full-blooded, both-feet-off-the ground jump that saw him landing on that cigarette packet with enough force to break a brick. The poor thing never had a chance. But Bonnke wasn't finished yet. He continued stomping, as other items, unrecognisable from my position on the balcony, were thrown under his feet. Then he walked across the stage. 'God is still telling me that someone here has an occult object to get rid of,' he said. A second or so went by. And then, just as he expected, up it came. Bonnke stomped with joy.

"I admit, my reactions as I left the Centre were mixed. I categorised the experience as a culture-shock - a little piece of Africa had found its way to Melbourne, and I'd been unprepared for it. No doubt back across the Indian Ocean, Bonnke's approach is perfectly appropriate. Yet despite my discomfort, I found myself admiring a man who was prepared to go out on a limb, to stick to what he sensed God was telling him, even if he ran the risk of looking a fool. Moreover, I was sure, despite my scruples, that people had done real business with God. I had little doubt that some had been freed from bondage to smoking, and to the occult. I believed this because I knew that such liberation comes because God's power locks in behind faith - whatever outward expression that might take.

"I had the chance to interview Bonnke and I asked him if he experienced the same enthusiastic response in western countries as he does in Africa?"

'No,' he admitted. 'I believe the reason for this is that God's harvest fields are not all ripe at the same time. It seems to me that there is a rotation in this matter, and I believe that this is God's hour for Africa'.

"Is there, then, something that makes Africans more in tune with God's Spirit?"

'Africans do seem to find it easier to put their trust in Jesus. They hear the Word, put their faith in it and it happens.'

"Well, what stops it happening in the West?"

'I believe the origin of our unbelief is western education. At great expense and effort, it reshapes our minds in the opposite direction to the Word of God. Then we say, we cannot believe in something that can't be proved - like the Word of God.'

"Yet Bonnke still insists God is capable of breaking down western prejudices. One way, he believes, is through trusting Him for 'signs and wonders'.

'It's as old as the Acts of the Apostles, it's the ministry of Jesus. It's simply a matter of returning to the original pattern. The idea - often expressed to me by Westerners - that it's a question of mentality, is utter nonsense and I resent it!

'I was preaching last year in Zurich and right in the front row was a lady who had been confined to a wheelchair for 20 years. I was preaching the Word of

God - I hadn't prayed at all for the sick yet - and suddenly she stood up. She was walking and crying! Lots of people present knew her and her illness and those people went nuts! The stiff Swiss! No, it's not a question of mentality. When God moves, people move, no matter what culture.

'If God's people are bold enough to speak in line with the Word of God, God proves His own Word. None of us needs to defend the Almighty. A lion needs no defence. Just open the cage!' "

"I'd seen enough to know he was basically right. I wanted to tell myself it's easier said than done, but I couldn't help feeling ... well ... uncomfortable. Again. But not this time, about the style of a visiting Bible thumper. I was finding out how disconcerting it can be to come face to face with a man who takes God absolutely seriously. In the end, returning to the 'original pattern' of the early church has to be an all-or-nothing exercise ..." (excerpts from *On Being*, November issue 1985).

In December, Reinhard, accompanied by Pastor Ray McCauley, of Rhema Ministries South Africa, stopped over in Perth, Western Australia, for a two-day rally before continuing on to Singapore. The headlines of the daily newspaper *The West Australian*, summed up the visit: BONNKE SHAKES PERTH.

A total of 23 churches and local fellowships combined to rent the "Entertainment Centre" where up to 7,000 people attended each night. Hundreds made first-time decisions for the Lord.

"Even though the crusade was so short it was the best we have ever had in Perth," said local organiser Pastor Brian Baker. "It is the first time that so many churches in this city have co-operated. That's a miracle in itself," he added.

On the second evening of the rally there was an outstanding miracle, which not only shook those in the centre, but made major headlines in the media the following day.

While preaching Reinhard approached a woman sitting in a wheelchair and told her he had a Word from the Holy Spirit that she was going to be healed during the service. "Do you believe that?" asked Reinhard. The woman's head slumped onto her chest - her faith was too weak to give a positive reply.

It was an extremely bold moment, but earlier in the day Reinhard had been assured by the Holy Spirit that the Lord was going to heal a woman in a green sweater. When his eyes fell on the woman in the wheelchair, wearing a green top, he knew this was the person that Jesus was going to heal that night.

A wave of faith flowed through Reinhard, filling him with a holy audacity that surprised him. He took the woman by the hand and began to pray for her. Then, with a hushed audience looking on, told her to stand up in the name of Jesus.

In that moment it happened - the power of God shot into her limbs! She jumped out of the wheelchair - totally healed. It was almost impossible to quieten the crowd who began rejoicing and praising God for this miracle. The woman, 34-year-old Shirley McKelt, had been told by doctors that she would possibly never walk again, but in that glorious moment God had done what was impossible for man!

It so happened that a Perth Channel Nine television crew was at the meeting and filmed this dramatic healing as it happened. It was shown nationwide the following day. There was also a clip of film showing Reinhard laughing and smiling as he was wheeled across the stage in Mrs McKelt's wheelchair!

Local newspaper reporters visited Mrs McKelt the next day and stated: "Mrs McKelt opened the front door herself ... her wheelchair stood folded in the hall."

Pastor Baker followed up this healing and later sent CFAN a letter with a doctor's report which indicated that initially Mrs McKelt had broken the neck of the femur bone and was unable to walk. She had an operation two weeks prior to going to the meeting, but was still unable to walk. After the meeting she had an X-ray and these showed new bone growth, which normally should have taken ten weeks. Stiffness in muscle and nerves went and the doctors gave her an "excellent report."

Less than four weeks later Reinhard was again bound for 'Down Under', his destination this time was the South Australian capital of Adelaide where he shared the platform with, among others, Paul Yonggi Cho, of South Korea. Reinhard was speaking at the annual United Charismatic Convention, organised by Barry Chant, who had invited Reinhard to attend this convention when he had first met him at the tent dedication in February 1984.

It was a convention during which Reinhard again displayed tremendous boldness, which amazed the people and which he admitted to me on his return got him into a spot of trouble as well. He and Brother Cho had been swopping stories about healing and how predictions sometimes went awry. Brother Cho told him of an occasion when he had prayed for dozens of people once while preaching in Finland. When he returned a few years later everyone expected more miracles and so did he. But nothing happened!

One afternoon Reinhard felt sure that the Lord

had given him a word concerning a sick person in the auditorium - but nothing happened! It's a measure of Reinhard's character that he didn't try to make any excuses. "I missed it, but then I'm only human. I told the Lord I was sorry; 'Teach me Lord, I want to know where I went wrong ... I want to learn.' "

As part of the convention and as an outreach to Adelaide permission was obtained to hold an open air meeting in the city centre, in Victoria Square - but it was limited to one hour. Reinhard was given the honour of preaching and many came forward to accept Jesus. Overlooking Victoria Square is the Hilton Hotel and staying there was a visiting Canadian businessman, who heard the gospel from his bedroom window and gave his life to Jesus as well.

"I was staying at the same hotel and he came and told me about his decision and joined the delegates at the conference for the rest of the week," explained Reinhard.

Another poignant example of the power of the gospel to reach into the heart of man, whether in a mass meeting or alone in a hotel bedroom in a foreign city.

Chapter 14

Moving Base

THE year 1985 must rank as the most traumatic for Reinhard - and for the team. Sure there'd been the drama of losing the Big Tent the previous year, but this was nothing compared with what would unfold in 1985.

Firstly, there was the move into genuine mass evangelism. There was the tragic death of two colleagues. There was also a momentous decision to uproot from South Africa and it was this latter decision which caused the most serious upheaval for all, including the Bonnkes. It forced many of the CFAN team to quit and even caused some confusion for Christians in South Africa.

But none of these events or decisions were apparent to anyone when departmental heads met in the new year, on January 11th, 1985. It was a routine meeting, discussing the mundane matters that apply to the efficient running of any organisation.

Some attention was given to finances and the need to budget wisely and Reinhard, who attended the meeting, shared some of his plans for the future. He warned of the difficulties that would be encountered; lower living standards, dangers of disease and generally harsher conditions for the crusade team. He expressed a strong desire for each man to duplicate himself in his specific area of expertise and to strive for greater efficiency.

He expressed an intention to build up the CFAN Village as a multi-racial community and strongly advised that the women and children remain at home while the men were up north on crusades. There was talk of securing a large plane, which would ferry the men to and from the crusades, giving them adequate time off to be at home with their families.

I believe we all left the meeting feeling that our futures looked reasonably secure. Little did we know what would transpire when we next met in eight weeks time on March 8th.

Besides a series of international speaking engagements Reinhard, accompanied by Peter, decided to spy out the land further north into Africa. They travelled to six countries on the West Coast, including: Togo, the Ivory Coast, Nigeria, Cameroons, Ghana and Upper Volta. They gained valuable information and established some vital new contacts. But what they discovered was that CFAN's connections with South Africa were potentially a far greater hindrance than they had ever considered.

Reinhard, during his travels overseas and into Africa, had often faced a barrage of hostile questions from the media, concerning South Africa. His answer is always that he regards himself as a preacher of the Good News, and part of the solution. This is indeed true. Unfortunately, some of the antagonism and naked hatred expressed towards anything remotely connected with South Africa, was forceably brought home to Reinhard and Peter during their West Africa reconnaisance.

In Lagos they were told that people threw back gospel tracts if they saw they were printed in Pretoria. It became apparent that there was no way that the

South African members of the team would be allowed to travel in Africa with their present passports. And so on his return to Witfield Reinhard bluntly told the staff that he had come to a realistic conclusion that if they were to win Africa for Jesus, they could not stay in South Africa.

He announced immediate steps to downgrade the South African office and to register one in Harare, Zimbabwe. He warned that South African staff would have to obtain other passports if they wished to remain with CFAN.

Events began to happen swiftly. Fortunately CFAN had maintained an office in Harare since 1984 and was now the main centre for the planning of the massive FIRE Conference, which was to be held in the Sheraton Centre.

Staff and equipment had been flowing between Witfield and Harare for some months and a good circle of contacts had been established in the Zimbabwean capital. A major concern, though, was over the South African members of the team.

Reinhard reiterated time and again that they would have to obtain some other passport and this would be the responsibility of the individuals concerned. Reinhard, at a meeting on March 20th, asked everyone to be open and honest with regard to their desires to travel north. He added CFAN would do their best to help those who couldn't go north to find alternative employment.

The number of key South African personnel at that time was considerable. They included Kobus de Lange, head of the technical team, chief electrician Milton Kasselman (later killed in Zambia), associate evangelists Kenneth Meshoe and Adam Mtsweni, crusade director Chris Lodewyk, Suzette Hattingh, with her vital intercessory ministry, Reinhard's long-time gospel soloist, Tommy Saaiden and other ministry, technical and administrative staff, who although not all key personnel, were nevertheless, very much part of the team.

For these South Africans, and I was among them, it became a mountainous problem. Initially, the South Africans did nothing. There was little they could do. There were crusades on the go and the ministry had to continue to function. It was also difficult to forecast when the move to Harare would be finalised.

By the end of April it was announced that CFAN intended to purchase a block of flats in Harare and by June this had been accomplished. It was obvious that the move to Harare would be sooner than some people at first expected. Some of the South African members began to make enquiries about immigrating to Zimbabwe in a legal attempt to get citizenship and a new passport.

However, to do this they would have to be resident in Zimbabwe for a period of at least five years before qualifying for a Zimbabwean passport. This, of course, was not feasible. Firstly, because the crusade team would continually be on the move in Africa and secondly, there was no guarantee that CFAN would be based in Zimbabwe for five years.

The South Africans were now faced with an agonising decision. Unless there was a miraculous change of heart, politically, in South Africa which made their passports acceptable, they would all have to leave.

Some stoically reached the decision and began to earnestly seek the Lord and plan for the future. Some resigned during the second half of the year. Others chose to remain with the team, for as long as possible, praying for a miracle, or hoping that Big Tent crusades would, for a time, be confined to those African nations still willing to accept South African passports.

It was, indeed, a trying period for all of those involved, who had not only their own futures to consider but also the future of their children, as regards schooling and education.

The decision to downgrade the Witfield office in South Africa and to establish Harare as the Africa base (for an unspecified time because it was apparent that the Africa base would eventually move northwards), also forced another decision - the need for an international headquarters.

Offices existed in West Germany, USA and Britain and it was decided that the international head-quarters should be in Europe because of the ease with which it is able to fly to most of the capitals of Africa from Europe. There was a momentary debate about whether it should be Britain or West Germany, but, for obvious reasons, Reinhard voted for Germany! And so a search began for a suitable base in West Germany.

In November 1985, Reinhard was in Frankfurt and made some enquiries about a property. One caught his attention. It had good grounds, offices and several apartments. It was close to the city and, of vital importance, close to the international airport at Frankfurt. The price also looked keen because the property was being sold by a bank, who had seized it after the owners had gone insolvent.

Reinhard made an offer and took an option on the property. At a meeting in Witfield on November 26th, at which he asked the team to pray for the Frankfurt property, he confidently predicted that

CFAN would clinch the deal, at a good price. A few weeks later a deal was struck. CFAN now had its international headquarters.

Meanwhile, the moving of personnel and equipment to Harare had already begun in full swing by mid-1985. It was estimated that the CFAN vehicle fleet would have to take 35 loads of equipment to Harare, a distance of 1,100 km. Staff began moving into the apartments in Harare, where momentum was being gained for the FIRE conference, now postponed to April 1986, and for the Big Tent crusade which was to run in conjunction with the international conference.

These three factors, the moving (and all its attendant implications), the conference and the Big Tent crusade preparation, put an unbelievable strain on CFAN's limited human and financial resources. At the same time expansion was occurring with the purchase of the Frankfurt base and also the establishment of a West African base.

As the changes began to develop so a strategy began to emerge. The new Big Tent, which would be ready and in action in April 1986, would concentrate on crusades in southern and central Africa, with a mobile team operating from a base in Nigeria, organising open air meetings there and in neighbouring countries.

The West African base was to be established by the seasoned and astute CFAN loyalist Winfried Wentland and his wife Gabi. He would have a complete sound system, a platform, lights and truck and he would be in charge of the technical arrangements for all the West African Crusades.

From Harare plans would be made to reach across into Malawi, Tanzania, Uganda and Kenya with the

Big Tent. The move into Africa was no longer talk - it was happening and much faster than anyone anticipated.

At one meeting Reinhard had hoped that the final move to Harare would be completed by the end of 1986. As it turned out the Witfield complex officially closed on May 31st, 1986.

By then most of the South African staff had come to a final decision. Singer Tommy Saaiden left late in 1985 to pioneer a church in Cape Town. Adam Mtsweni took over a church in the Black area of Tembesa, on the East Rand. Kenneth Meshoe was staying on until the end of 1986, and then leaving for the USA to further his studies at Bible school.

Chris Lodewyk, who had planned to start up a Christian travel service, was asked to stay on as international crusade and conference director based in Frankfurt, although it was understood that he would not be able to travel to events in Africa.

Kobus de Lange and Suzette Hattingh are continuing until the end of 1986, and will only then make a final decision as to where their futures lie.

For the South Africans it has been a traumatic decision. I speak from personal experience because, like most, I had hoped that somehow I would be able to remain, possibly based in Germany. However, this was not possible and it was with a deep sadness that I had to face the fact that my season with CFAN had come to an end.

I was greatly encouraged, though, by a word that Reinhard shared at a meeting I attended. He said: "There is no demotion in the Kingdom of God ... only promotion." It struck me forcibly because it was my natural, human desire to want to cling to CFAN. My almost four-year association with

Reinhard and the team had been the best, most exciting and most rewarding spiritual years of my whole life. But the Holy Spirit spoke those words through Reinhard's lips and I realised that the next few years are going to be even grander! But I had to let go and that, I think, has been the toughest hurdle for the South Africans to overcome.

Several other staff members left during the course of the year, and others stayed on until May 31st to see through the Harare conference and crusade. Several of these, too, have decided to go into the ministry. So although there has been a certain sadness and upheaval, it has in fact, been most beneficial to the Kingdom of God.

Like all dynamic ministries CFAN has drawn some top class people, who have developed and matured greatly from their experience with an evangelist like Reinhard. And eventually the time arrives when the "eaglets" have to leave the nest and fly by themselves. That, I believe, is what God has accomplished through the unfortunate upheaval that came to the staff.

The scaling down of CFAN's operation in South Africa has, unfortunately, been misinterpretated by some White Christians in South Africa and Reinhard's decision likened to running away from the trouble and unrest which exploded in South Africa during 1985/86. Many believe he should remain in South Africa and continue to preach there, in an effort to bring about a change of heart that will stop the violence.

However, Reinhard's priority has never been South Africa. His calling has always been to Africa. South Africa is only a small part of that vision. There is a whole continent to be reached and Reinhard is not prepared to prejudice his commission and call for the sake of any political ideology or to keep a selfish few White Christians cozy in their beds at night!

Reinhard has steered clear of political storms. He is vehemently opposed to apartheid but has never used the pulpit to pontificate to political leaders, whether on the Right, Left or Centre. His message centres on Jesus Christ, the only way of true peace and reconciliation.

Reinhard is prepared to preach in the capital of the "racist Pretoria regime," or in Red Square, Moscow, and confound atheism, or in capitalistic Washington. Wherever there are sinners you'll find Reinhard proclaiming the power of the gospel to change lives and attitudes. That's why his statement, "I'm part of the solution", is no glib press comment. He believes that there is only one solution to the world's complex problems and that is Jesus Christ.

CFAN will however maintain a small office in South Africa, which will handle correspondence and distribute video and audio tapes and maintain a link with the thousands of faithful prayer partners, who share the vision to see Africa won for Jesus. That will be its only function. All of the central administration will be controlled from Frankfurt, with close co-operation with the offices in West Africa and Zimbabwe, or later on, Nairobi.

By the end of 1986 the last of the South African passport holders will have left the Africa team and Reinhard's links will almost all be severed with the "deep south". Fortunately, a large number of the prayer partners in South Africa do appreciate the expediency of CFAN establishing its bona fides in Africa and will continue to pray and support the ministry, even though it will be at long distance.

Chapter 15

To Sell or
Not to Sell

AN immediate question that arose when the move from South Africa was first mooted was what would become of the Witfield complex? And what at first may have been a simple question turned into a controversial issue, with many people shaking their heads in bewilderment.

It's been a decision that has caused people to wonder what the Lord's will really was in the matter and it's been a difficult issue to explain. Thus I have devoted a separate chapter to the controversy, in an attempt to give the background and the full story of how Witfield was eventually sold and why.

In June 1985, Reinhard told a departmental meeting that several parties had expressed interest in purchasing the Witfield complex and he gave every indication that he would sell as soon as possible.

At a departmental meeting, a month later, he told the staff that he would be sending out a letter to various Christian ministries explaining his decision to sell the property. I was involved in preparing a letter with a description of the property and this letter was due to be posted on Monday, July 29th. Reinhard was away for the weekend spending some time in fellowship with several other ministers in Durban.

On his return he came straight to my office informing me that the letter was to be scrapped. He was not going to sell the property - he was going to give it away. He then prepared another letter which was sent to all CFAN prayer partners in which he outlined his crusade plans and also shared with them his vision for the future of Witfield. In the letter he said, concerning the property:

"We have received a very clear word from God to move our main base to Europe where we will be able to reach the countries in question with greater ease. Our base at Witfield will be closed. I had intended selling it so as to be in a position to purchase a replacement overseas, but the Lord clearly spoke to me that I should not do so. This base will become a centre for intercession and fasting, so that "the angel of death" will be stopped in Africa. We have taken this decision in obedience to the Word of the Lord. To take this step is not easy, because we desperately needed the money of the Witfield base to establish the new one. I am throwing myself, with my team, into the arms of the Lord. He will see us through. Please pray for us." This letter was dated August 6th, 1985.

When this decision was announced it was met with a gasp. It was surely a magnanimous gesture, giving away a property worth $500,000. Some of the staff rejoiced. They believed it was the right decision and witnessed with it. Others still believed that the property should be sold. To Christians outside it was a breath-taking decision and greatly admired. The big question which now arose was: who would get the property?

Reinhard stated that he wanted it to go to a ministry that had a vision for Africa to be saved. He'd expressed the hope that it would become a centre for prayer, fasting, teaching and intercession - a hub for many facets of evangelism and missions - with a view to unity for all in Africa. He added that he was prepared to turn over the property, with no strings attached, except that the facility becomes a point of unity to pray and reach the rest of Africa.

The word soon spread through the country. Telephone calls and letters came in from many ministries and individuals. Almost everyone believed, emphatically, that the Lord had given them a word for the property! Such is the folly of zealous charismatics!

The months drifted by and no decision was reached. One or two people put forward plans to make use of the complex, but it became apparent that there was no ministry with the financial muscle and size capable of making full use of the property.

Schemes for sharing the complex among several ministries were put forward, but none were satisfactory. When this was mentioned somebody remarked that Witfield would become an "ecclesiastical refugee camp"! It now seemed that the apparently simple thing of giving the property away was, in fact, pitted with spikey problems.

There was Reinhard's denominational affiliation, which honestly felt they should be in the running. There were also some close minister friends, who felt Reinhard might pass it their way.

And so he found himself in a position whereby his gift had become an offence. Clearly by giving it to one person or group was going to hurt others, who felt they should have received it!

Reinhard wrestled with the puzzle. His first inclination was to sell. Then he was convinced that the Lord told him to give it away. But now the saints were squabbling over the gift. Could he go back on what he had so boldly stated and written? Could he sell? Would he be disobeying the Lord? In February 1986 I remember meeting him in the driveway at Witfield and asking him whether he had come to a decision yet.

"No, not yet. I haven't decided," was his reply.

I turned and said to him: "Reinhard, do what your heart is telling you to do. Give it to the one that is on your heart."

He nodded, but didn't reply. I think that what was in his heart then was to sell, but he hadn't yet got the greenlight from the Lord.

Then the greenlight came. It came from a close friend and a pastor, who is regarded as a man of high integrity and a man who knows the voice of the Lord. The man was Rev. Ed Roebert, of Pretoria.

The scriptural backing for the reversal of the decision was based on Abraham's willingness to sacrifice his only son Isaac. The Witfield complex had been Reinhard's "Isaac". He had laid it down on the altar and God was allowing him to pick it up again and sell it.

Reinhard breathed a sigh of relief. It confirmed what he believed. Of course, the change of decision rocked many people, who began to doubt whether Reinhard really heard from the Lord. Understandable for those not in possession of all the facts.

Next step was to contact several ministries, who had shown interest and ask them whether they wanted to buy the property. But there were no takers. Next was to advertise in the secular press, Reinhard having now abandoned the concept of at least seeing Witfield sold to a Christian.

Then contact was made with Jan de Rouwe, a wealthy businessman, who is also senior pastor of the East Rand Christian Centre. Jan is a long-time supporter of CFAN. Yes, Jan was interested. His desire, for many years, has been to start a Christian school. The Witfield complex would suit this ideally because not only did it have offices, accommodation, a swimming pool and tennis court, but plenty of vacant ground for further development.

After a close inspection Jan made a cash offer, which was not accepted. However, a couple of weeks later, during the FIRE Conference in Harare, Reinhard, Peter and Jan sat down and finalised a sale, which included the selling of Reinhard's own house, as part of the deal. The property saga was over.

Chapter 16

Fire Across Africa

WHEN the all-Africa conference on evangelism was first mentioned by Reinhard, the number of delegates envisaged was 600 or 700. The initial venue was to have been Swaziland. Later this was switched to Harare, Zimbabwe. The dates also changed. First it was late 1984, then it was moved to 1985 and eventually finalised for April 1986. By then the size of the conference and the importance had become truly international.

There were 4,000 delegates, nearly 1,000 of them sponsored, and some of the world's finest speakers were invited to the conference. For Inter-African Revival Evangelists, a name which had to be contrived to spell out FIRE - of the Holy Spirit.

When Reinhard first got the idea for the conference, there was no one in CFAN capable of organising such an event. There was speculation of hiring an outside agency to plan and execute the conference, but as so often happens though, Reinhard did not let the finer details of the project bother him. If God had ordained the event then He would provide the wherewithall, including personnel and finances. He did.

As mentioned earlier, one of the "finds" of the Cape Town Crusade was organiser Chris Lodewyk and it was upon him that the responsibility fell. God could not have sent a better equipped man for putting together what was to prove Chris's toughest-ever assignment.

In fact, there are probably few professional conference planners who would have attempted the task, especially with the small staff, restricted budget, and CFAN's lack of experience in planning an international event. What Chris did in getting the CFAN staff geared up for the event and handling multiple complications, was often amazing.

A man of lesser fortitude would have thrown up his hands in despair and said it was impossible. By the grace of God and sheer hard work and long hours Chris and his small team deservedly won the plaudids of all for a spectacular success.

It's hard for westerners to appreciate the difficulties encountered in organising events in Africa. Fortunately CFAN has gained this experience from its crusade planning and Chris was forewarned about some of the obstacles he would encounter.

One major difficulty is communication systems within Africa. Telephones are apt to go out of order regularly. Telexes are not as plentiful as one would wish. Letter delivery services are also unreliable. That was obstacle number one.

Because there is so much poverty in Africa it was obvious that many of the evangelists would have to be sponsored, partly, or fully. This immediately raised the problem of selection. It would not be difficult to find preachers wanting to be sponsored, but CFAN did not want to waste money on conference hoppers, or on men who had no real calling or vision in their ministries.

This meant trying to establish contact with reputable men of God in each nation in Africa. This was no easy job. Open-minded, men of integrity, had to be found. Men who have a vision for the kingdom of God and not those interested only in building up their own empires. The contacts had to be men with a vision for their nation and for Africa.

To achieve this meant sending men into Africa, travelling extensively to meet and spy out the land. Among those engaged in this task were Werner Drotleff and Ekkehard Hornburg, both of CFAN and Mike Oman, Youth With a Mission director in Zimbabwe. Thousands of applications were received and then came the drawn out process of examining each one and checking out references - which took months and months because of the poor communications within Africa.

Another obstacle was transportation. Once the delegates were selected the next step was to co-ordinate their travel from their homes to Harare. Many were able to come by road from neighbouring countries, like Mozambique, Malawi, Zambia, Zaire, Lesotho, Swaziland, Botswana and South Africa. For those further north it meant taking a flight. This is easier said than done.

Most African nations have their own internal flights, but international flights are mainly confined to the major airlines, operating from Europe. At one stage it looked as though some delegates would be better off flying to London and then back to Harare.

As it turned out many delegates had to catch at least four connecting flights in order to get to Harare. To help, CFAN chartered several flights. One of these went to Lagos, which became a central meeting place on the West Coast, and another flew to Nairobi, on the East African coast.

Even then unforeseen things happened. The Lagos

charter was impounded by airport officials because certain fees had not been paid. Fortunately, Mike Oman had accompanied the flight to Lagos and after making representation to some of the highest authorities, including the chief of the airforce, the matter was resolved. The fees had been paid, but someone had put their "hand in the till". Corruption, unfortunately, is another obstacle one encounters in many parts of Africa.

Then there was the question of immigration and customs, applications for visas and the importing of goods and equipment for the running of the conference. Key personnel, who worked closely with Chris were an American couple Bud and Doris Horton, who had given up their own business in the USA to join CFAN.

Another vital link was Chris Alberts, a Zimbabwean, who carried the heavy responsibility of negotiating with the customs and immigration authorities.

All of CFAN, of course, were engaged in certain areas of the conference and there was wonderful support from dozens of volunteers from Harare itself.

Accommodation was another area. Altogether 22 Hotels were booked, while hundreds of Christians opened their homes to those who could not afford to pay for hotels. All of this had to be financed. And finance was one realm where a miracle was needed.

Because of Reinhard's commitment to crusades and to the moving of bases across the world, money became exceptionally tight. In fact, Reinhard admits that in mid-January he came very close to postponing the conference because response, at that time, had been luke-warm and finances were low.

He flew with Peter to consult with Chris and as

they discussed the problems, "the Spirit of God came on me and a soothing peace flooded me," recalls Reinhard. Chris told him he needed urgently Zim $400,000. Reinhard promised he would get it to him within a week. And he did! God provided!

From an organisational aspect the conference was a huge success. So much so that the Zimbabwean Government asked Chris to advise them on certain aspects for a forthcoming conference of Non-Aligned States! But the greatest success of the conference, was indeed, spiritual.

The speakers were of the highest calibre and represented various flows and ministries within the Kingdom of God. There was Loren Cunningham, founder of Youth With a Mission - Kenneth and Gloria Copeland, Wayne Myers, from Mexico, Ralph Mahoney, founder of World Mission Assistance Plan, Bishop Benson Idahosa, from Nigeria, Dr Ron Shaw, from India, Dr Robert Schuller, of the famous Crystal Cathedral in California and from South Africa Elijah Maswanganyi, Ray McCauley, Ed Roebert and Nicky van der Westhuizen. Reinhard Bonnke and Suzette Hattingh were also speakers.

The theme of the conference was evangelism and every aspect of it and these gifted speakers made a valuable and lasting contribution to the vision and commission for the salvation of Africa.

Altogether 41 African nations, including some of the Indian Ocean islands, were represented at the conference. There were also visitors, from America, Britain, West Germany, Norway, Sweden, Denmark, France, Singapore and Australia.

From the outset Reinhard stated that the prime reason for the conference was to set aflame a spark in the hearts of God's servants that they would each go back to their village, town, and city and set their nation alight for Jesus.

The conference stirred the hearts of all who were there. It visibly demonstrated unity within the Body of Christ. Reinhard has never shown partiality towards denominations and this was not a consideration when screening applications. So, men and women, from a variety of denominations and various ministries, found themselves thrust together in Harare.

The Holy Spirit did a glorious job of welding them together and showing them the folly of artificial barriers which divided. If unity was a strong force at work, so too, of course, was evangelism. The speakers challenged the delegates time and again and to widen their vision and their expectations. A strident call from the conference was, in fact, to accept the challenge to change nations by the power of the gospel.

Since the conference hundreds of letters have poured into the Harare office, telling of the fires lit in the hearts of hundreds of delegates, and of their determination to put into practice what they learnt and saw at the conference. When the conference closed there were calls for a future conference of the same nature.

A special, and very different feature of the conference, was the fact that a crusade was held in conjunction with it. Nightly, delegates were able to go to the new Big Tent to see mass evangelism in action. For many it was a new dimension of ministry to see thousands responding to altar calls and see the power of God demonstrated when the sick were prayed for and healed.

A constant comment from delegates when they left Harare to return to their homes, was simply: "I'll never be the same again."

The FIRE conference was indeed a life-changing experience - even for Reinhard himself. As the host he spoke at the opening ceremony and gave the final address on the closing Saturday morning. That Saturday morning will never be forgotten by those who were there.

In the opulent conference centre, with the flags of 50 nations bedecking the balconies, the Holy Spirit moved in a powerful and mighty way, that saw Reinhard crumble to the floor under the anointing of the Spirit. The guest speakers surrounded him and prayed for him and evangelist Dave Newberry, brought a powerful prophecy which thundered through the centre.

The central theme of the prophecy was that a greater outpouring of God's Spirit was coming and that Reinhard would, in the name of Jesus, "subdue nations" and stand before "kings and rulers". The prophecy added that the Lord was gathering a "mighty army" which would undergird the CFAN ministry and this was, indeed, the "hour of a new move of the Holy Spirit in the world!"

The closing ceremony of the conference was a communion service, held in the Big Tent on Sunday morning. It was a touching service with close to 20,000 Christians sharing the bread and wine and remembering their mighty Saviour.

I spoke to many of the guest speakers and for most of them it was a unique experience. They all left Harare deeply touched by what God is doing in Africa, sensing that this is, indeed, the beginning of a great outpouring of the Holy Spirit upon the continent.

Kenneth Copeland was ecstatic about the conference and what he had observed: "We are approaching God's finest hour. We are seeing the salvation of a continent. I have seen things at the FIRE Conference which I have never experienced before. The atmosphere was charged with revival, faith and a unity that thrilled my heart. In fact, it's the greatest spirit of revival I've ever seen."

The esteemed founder of Youth With A Mission (YWAM), Loren Cunningham added this comment: "The first night when I heard Brother Bonnke declare 'Africa shall be saved', I was excited because I did not just hear the voice of a man, but the very heart cry of God. 'Africa shall be saved' is a statement of faith. The fire of God is touching lives, especially in the area of evangelism and healing."

This theme was echoed by Bishop Benson Idahosa, a long time campaigner in Africa: "This was a God-ordained event to lift us up. Our previous maximums became our minimums and we now look for greater things to happen. 'Africa shall be saved' is not a slogan. No, it's a reality. Men of God across the continent are going to begin to take united action to save Africa ... evangelist Bonnke is a precious gift ... a treasure to the people of Africa. I urge Christians to back him up with their prayers and support."

It was a wonderful personal triumph for Reinhard. A vindication, once again, of his faith and vision because there were times when the conference seemed doomed, either because of lack of finance, or because of the immense logistical (and political) difficulties involved with organising such an event in Africa. But the divine dream that was deposited in Reinhard's spirit late in 1983 was fulfilled. For those who were intimately involved in the long build-up to the event it was truly brought about by divine grace.

Reinhard summed up the event like this: "In the 19 years of evangelising in Africa I have never experienced such a mighty release of new gifts and anointings of the Holy Spirit. I believe we have reached a major turning point in Africa. I have always preached and believed that Africa shall be saved and this conference was a tangible step towards achieving this divine goal."

I believe that a lot of the success of the conference was due to the crusade meetings held in the new Big Tent because this gave delegates on-the-spot examples of campaign preaching. They saw Reinhard and others, like Benson Idahosa, Kenneth Copeland, Ray McCauley and Nicky van der Westhuizen, preaching and praying for the sick. As one delegate said afterwards it was like years of training all wrapped up in one week.

The crusade attracted thousands each night and by the time the meetings ended 8,600 first-time decisions were recorded. There were also multiple healings, which thrilled and excited the congregations each night.

The fact that the crusade was staged at all was a direct answer to prayer and a bouquet once again for Suzette Hattingh and her diligent team of intercessors.

From early on it had been planned to run the conference and crusade side by side, despite the heavy burden it presented for CFAN's limited resources. Once the Conference Centre had been booked, the next step was to find a crusade site which was fairly close to the Centre.

A site was found and permission granted by the

Harare City Council and the technical team immediately began work. This was to be the first erection of the new tent which was designed by a British firm and manufactured in West Germany. Although the basic design was maintained there were certain alterations and it was vital that the technical staff got an opportunity to do some tests before the crusade began.

In the meantime, some residents who lived near to the open fields where the tent was to be sited, began to raise objections, especially when they saw the size of the tent when it was raised. They were concerned about the influx of thousands of people and additional traffic into the area.

There then began a long drawn out series of objections, which eventually lead to a High Court injunction. The Harare City Council stuck to their guns, with CFAN giving assurances about noise and crowd control.

The court action dragged on and the final judgement, in favour of CFAN, came only days before the crusade began. It had been another attempt by Satan to halt the gospel but, as always, he was defeated. Again it had been a battle waged in the spirit realm with the intercessors in the frontline.

Chapter 17

The New Big Tent

WHEN the Big Tent was destroyed in Cape Town in May 1984, it was widely accepted that because it was insured it would only be a matter of six months or a little longer before a new tent roof was manufactured. However, it took 18 months before the Big Tent was again raised in Africa - and a financial miracle.

The insurance claim became bogged down in a series of technicalities and it became obvious that full payment was in doubt and that it would be a long drawn out affair. In the meantime, Reinhard was straining to get a new roof, but how to raise the money?

He confided in close friend Pastor Ray McCauley about his concern for a new tent roof and Ray promised to help in anyway he could when the two men flew to America on a brief speaking engagement. It was during this visit that God provided the money to pay for the new tent roof.

Reinhard and Ray paid a visit to Kenneth Copeland's ministry headquarters in Fort Worth, Texas. The three men met over breakfast in a city restaurant and began to discuss the needs of CFAN in its evangelistic crusades in Africa.

As the men shared openly with each other the Spirit of God suddenly intervened in the discussion. Reinhard and Ray stopped talking. Across the table

Kenneth Copeland, obviously under a powerful anointing of the Holy Spirit, spoke out boldly. What he said caused Reinhard's eyes to open in wide amazement.

"I'll pay for the new tent roof," were the words that fell from Copeland's lips, but they could have come directly from the Throne Room of the Almighty.

The atmosphere tingled with a holy fervency. The men looked at the plates of bacon and egg, which seemed so out of place as loud "hallelujahs!" punctuated the air, causing a few fellow diners to cast a querying eye at the three preachers, now lost in the glory of the Lord! God had spoken and that was all that mattered. A new tent roof was on the way and Reinhard could hardly wait to get back to the beloved land of Africa.

As the three men walked out into the bright sunlight Reinhard's eyes blazed with an ardent zeal. Indeed, Africa would be saved! The devil would never halt him in his holy crusade through Africa.

Unknown to Reinhard at the time though, was the fact that Kenneth Copeland Ministries was far from flush with money.

Speaking at the dedication of the new Big Tent in Harare, in April 1986, Copeland shared with the congregation how it had been a giant step of faith to promise to pay for the tent.

His ministry, he said, was almost $1-million behind in payments. He'd asked the Lord for a good place in which to sow finance and when he had met with Reinhard and Ray McCauley over breakfast, the Lord had moved on him. This was the opportunity to sow financially.

Believing beyond doubt that this was the Lord's leading, Copeland had pledged to pay the $800,000 needed to replace the tent roof.

When he told this story to the large audience in the tent in Harare he emphasised that, truly, Jesus had paid for the new roof.

"I never paid for it. Jesus paid for it," and as he gave the glory to God, the people erupted into a wave of praise and thanksgiving.

Because of small structural changes the profile of the new Big Tent has become more rounded and the interior space decreased slightly, although it will still seat close to 30,000 people. However, with the experiences gained in the open air crusades in West Africa it is more than likely that future Big Tent crusades will be standing room only. By eliminating the seating it will be possible to get close to 70,000 under cover.

Some people still wonder why a tent is needed, especially when Reinhard has enjoyed such large and spectacular success in open air meetings.

However, not all city authorities will give permission for outdoor meetings, claiming that it is a security risk. Sometimes it is not possible to obtain the use of stadiums. Then, of course, there is the weather. Heat and rain can make outdoor meetings very difficult, but the Big Tent provides good shelter from the elements.

Reinhard's Africa strategy is now based on a two-prong attack in Africa. One, by means of outdoor meetings on the West Coast and the second along the East Coast, using the Big Tent.

Already a base has been established in Ghana, on the West Coast, with a mobile team equipped with platform, floodlights and sound system. And not a street corner sized sound system. One thing Reinhard has always insisted on is excellent sound. "What's the good of people coming to a meeting if they cannot hear the message?" is his simple and obvious argument.

I remember being at a CFAN departmental meeting in June 1985 when discussion centred on the sound system that Winfried Wentland would have in West Africa. Winfried explained that the present system had the capacity to reach 400,000 people.

Unimpressed Reinhard looked across the room at the rest of the staff: "That may be too small ... I've had a glimpse of the crowd that no man can number!"

And so instructions were given for a sound system that was capable of reaching a crowd of one million people.

Of course, that may sound awfully presumptuous, but I believe that in the not too distant future he will be preaching to crowds of that magnitude.

It's difficult for Christians in Britain and America to appreciate just how open the people of Africa are to the gospel. But not just open. No, they are desperately hungry for the Word of God. And not only desperately hungry, but are readily accepting Christ by the thousands - and soon by the million!

The problem which faces the Church in Africa is how to cope with this mighty harvest. There is an acute shortage of well-trained pastors and this is where other ministries are needed, to follow up behind Reinhard and his team.

Despite the great harvesting opportunities the obstacles are still great and sometimes dangerous. Africa, besides the besetting scourge of poverty and famine, is a political melting pot. The very ingredients of poverty and starvation make the position of national leaders extremely precarious.

The forces of Islam and the insidious agents of

Marxism are also at work on the African continent. The stakes are high in Africa.

Various ideologies are contending for the minds of the masses, but for those with true spiritual perception Africa is simply a giant chessboard with the nations as pawns and the players the devil and the Church.

The Church has sometimes woefully failed in Africa, but God has raised up a man in Reinhard Bonnke who has the boldness to proclaim that "Africa shall be saved". Not by feeding programmes. Not by aid programmes. Not by politicians. Not by capitalism, nor by communism - but simply by the Blood of Jesus Christ.

While many Christians use tip-toe faith, Reinhard has learnt that to succeed in the Kingdom of God one needs to take giant leaps of faith.

The Big Tent was a giant leap of faith and so was the FIRE Conference. The present all-out thrust into Africa is another big step of faith. The move to centre his headquarters in Frankfurt is another major leap in faith.

Although Reinhard's priority is still Africa I believe that God has placed him in Europe for more than simple logistic reasons.

Already Reinhard is planning various conferences and campaigns for Europe. They are mostly still on the drawingboard, but I, for one, would not be surprised to one day see the Big Tent in Europe!

The harvest in Africa is ripe and Reinhard and his team are reaping with an ardent fury. He believes that Christ, the Prince of Peace, is Africa's only answer to its numerous and complex difficulties.

The people of Africa are eagerly embracing Christ as Saviour and it may well be that these very people become the evangelists to invade Europe in the next decade.

I feel that God has already established a bridgehead with Reinhard's centre in Frankfurt which will be a catalyst for the awakening of Europe in the next ten years.

One thing is certain, Reinhard will never turn his back on Africa. God called him to this great continent as a little boy and his heart's desire is to fulfil that sacred trust and to chase the vision: Africa shall be saved!

THE END

Capetown 1984
Big Tent Destroyed

Soweto 1984
(photo Betty Lore)

Crusade at Harare Showgrounds.
Zimbabwe 1984
(photo Chris Musaka)

Welcome at Ibadan, Nigeria 1985

205

Ibadan 1985
Child healed of limb disorder

Adam Mtswene smashing witchcraft fetishes

Lubumbashi, Zaire 1985

Child healed
Lubumbashi, Zaire 1985

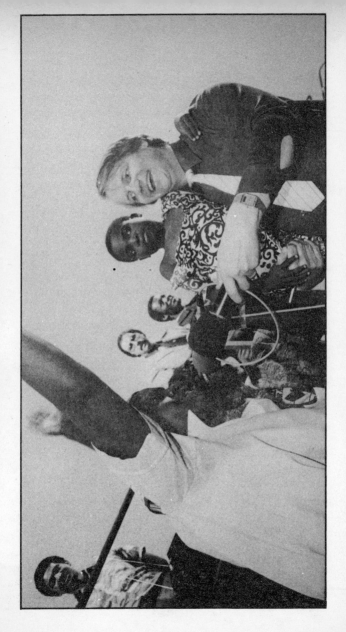

Crowds at Lubumbashi, Zaire 1985

Death Crash on Zambian Road
September 1985

Milton Kasselman and Horst Kossanke killed in road crash

Lusaka 1985

Also available from Sovereign World

How to receive the gifts of the Holy Spirit

Bill Subritzky

In this book the author explains with honesty, clarity and biblical precision how you can function effectively as a Spirit-gifted believer. Bridging the chasm between biblical instruction and spiritual function he covers:

* How every Christian can qualify to operate in the gifts
* Receiving the manifestational gifts of the Spirit
* The importance of practise in using the gifts
* Utilizing the biblical tools for spiritual discern-ment
* Love, the highest form of spiritual expression

Bill Subritzky lives in Auckland, New Zealand and travels extensively in his ministry.

112 pages   ISBN 1 85240 001 3

Demons defeated

Bill Subritzky

The author describes demons, who they are, their manifestations and how we can be delivered. He exposes the strong men, including Anti-christ, Death and Hell with their children and Jezebel.

He faces whether a Christian can have a demon, methods of deliverance and how to hold our deliverance. His ministry has taken him to many hundreds of thousands in meetings throughout Asia, North America and the South Pacific, and he has had to deal with many incidents involving deliverance. Bill Subritzky has held every position open to a lay person in the Church of England and lives in New Zealand.

276 pages   ISBN 1 85240 001 3

Free Indeed!

Tom Marshall

Many Christians find that there is a gap between what they know the Bible to say about freedom and what they actually experience. In this book the author emphasises that the gospel is for the whole man, spirit, soul and body and that biblical truth has to be applied in all these areas to experience the fulness of freedom and life in the Spirit which God intends for all believers. This book will help you to be transformed by the renewing of your mind and to be liberated into the freedom for which Christ died.

Tom Marshall is Senior Elder of the Kapiti Christian Centre, Raumati Beach, New Zealand and Managing Editor of the magazine *The Shaker*. He travels extensively in his Bible teaching ministry.

Large Format Illustrated.

208 Pages ISBN 1 85240 002 1

The Foundation Series

Derek Prince

A comprehensive Bible Foundation course
in Three Volumes

Volume One

Book One: Foundation for Faith
Book Two: Repent and Believe

Volume Two

Book Three: From Jordan to Pentecost
Book Four: Purposes of Pentecost

Volume Three

Book Five: Laying on of Hands
Book Six: Resurrection of the dead
Book Seven: Eternal Judgement

Further information about all Sovereign World titles can be obtained from any of the following addresses:

Sovereign World (N.Z.) Ltd.,
P.O. Box 24086,
Royal Oak,
AUCKLAND,
New Zealand.

Sovereign World (Australia) Ltd.,
6 Wambiri Place,
CROMER 2099,
N.S.W.
Australia.

Sovereign World (Singapore) Ltd.,
The Garden Hotel,
14 Balmoral Road,
SINGAPORE 1025.

Sovereign World (UK) Ltd.,
P.O. Box 17,
Chichester PO20 6RY
England.

Books are normally supplied through bookshops. How ever, in the case of difficulty, please send payment to the appropriate address above and copies will be posted to you. Allow an extra 10% for postage. If you would like details of the Sovereign World Trust which sends books into Third World countries please write for a brochure to:

Sovereign World Trust,
P.O. Box 777
Tonbridge,
Kent TN9 2RU
England